LUMBERJACK

LUMBERJACK

ADVENTURE IS CALLING
THE HISTORY, THE LORE, THE LIFE

Lauren Jarvis

AMMONITE
PRESS

CONTENTS

LUMBERJACKS: A HISTORY

Armed with axes and saws, the people who worked in the forests of North America changed the continent's historical, geographical and cultural landscape forever

They are a young and powerfully built race of men... generally unmarried and, though rude in manner and intemperate, are quite intelligent,' described author and explorer Charles Lanman in his 1856 book *Adventures in the Wilds of the United States and British American Provinces*. 'They seem to have a passion for their wild and toilsome life and, judging from their dress, I should think possess a fine eye for the comic and fantastic. The entire apparel of an individual consists of a pair of grey pantaloons and two red flannel shirts, a pair of long boots and a wool covering for the head, and all these things are worn at one and the same time.'

While these observations could have been made at a taco truck in Tacoma, or a gin distillery in Dalston, these flannel-wearing menfolk aren't hipsters, millennials or 'yuccies'. They are icons from another age, striding out of the forests and into eternity with shredded arms, steely eyes and wielding a sharpened axe. Built of substance over style, they're a rare, real deal; teasing the nose with notes of winter and woodsmoke that could be bottled and sold by Tom Ford. Men who've become myth, loggers who've become legend: lumberjacks.

SPIRIT OF ADVENTURE

Just like the cowboy, the lumberjack still permeates popular culture today. As with their Wild West cousins, these iconic figures have endured for their strength, work ethic and resilience – as well as those timelessly stylish plaid shirts.

Immortalised in books, films and

NAME CHECK

The first known mention of the word 'lumberjack' was in Canada's *Cobourg Star* newspaper in 1831, while the 'lumberjill' emerged during World War II. Other terms include 'shanty boy', 'brush monkey' or 'woodcutter', while modern lumberjacks are known as 'loggers' or 'timber cutters'.

A lumberjack standing at the base of a huge tree showing a cut in the tree, US, ca. 1900.

songs, their unmistakeable look has been adopted and adapted from one generation to the next, while their pioneering spirit of adventure and connection to the great outdoors continues to inspire urban warriors to return to the woods.

The 'young and powerfully built race of men' described by Lanman hailed from Maine, and their 'toilsome life' is that of a logger, felling trees deep in the forests of New England during the height of the lumber boom in 19th-century North America.

BUILDING THE NEW WORLD

From the moment the first permanent English settlement was established in 1607 in Jamestown, Virginia, the continent's forests became its most valued resource. Trees were cut for timber to build homes and make wagons that would roll across the Great Plains to the West, while woodlands were cleared for villages and farms. The best lumber was reserved for the Crown and sent to England to make naval ship masts: a contentious issue which was to play a part in the American Revolution. Forested states met a growing demand throughout the 1800s, with white pine the favoured wood to build their new America.

Early logging camps were run by family outfits, but in the 1820s larger lumber cooperatives gained control. Pennsylvania's forests were plundered, while in

New York additional land was granted to settlers who established sawmills, and its rivers flowed with logs on their way to meet them. By the 1830s, Bangor in Maine had become the world's largest shipping port for lumber, and logging crews were felling the monumental trees of America's Pacific Northwest and the pine forests of Canada.

In the mid-1800s, the process of turning wood pulp into paper came into play, which – along with mass immigration to America, the Civil War, the California Gold Rush, the rise of the railroads and the grinding wheels of the Industrial Revolution – turned out to be bad news for trees, if not the timber barons.

LOGGING LEGACY

Despite being built on their breaking backs, few of the profits from the logging boom made it into the calloused hands of the lumberjacks wielding the axe or bucking the logs. Life in the lumber camps was hard. Working in isolated forests through the harsh winter months, lumberjacks slept in ice-cold, crowded bunkhouses – and pay was poor.

Long before chainsaws and harvesters were invented, even the biggest of trees were felled by hand; the name 'misery whip' accurately described the discomfort of spending hours, days and months wielding a crosscut saw. Prior to steamboats and railroads, drivers

RISKY BUSINESS
Despite advances in machinery, working conditions and regulations, logging is still one of the most dangerous jobs in the world. The US Bureau of Labor Statistics' annual 2019 report on fatal occupational injuries places logging workers at number two, behind fishing and hunting workers and ahead of aircraft pilots and flight engineers.

risked being crushed or drowned as they guided and rode logs along rumbling rivers to the sawmills each spring on the 'log drive'. Camaraderie, good humour and strength – inner and outer – got them through.

From these remote camps and wild frontiers, the legendary lumberjacks Paul Bunyan and Big Joe Mufferaw were born. But it's the passionate, 'intemperate' loggers of the lumber woods who truly left their indelible mark on North America.

WOMEN IN CAMP

Lumber camps were almost exclusively men-only zones but by the late 1800s some women worked in the camps, usually as cooks or assistants, known as 'cookees' or 'flunkeys'. They would prep the meals, fire up the stoves, wait on tables and prepare lunches for men to take into the woods.

During the World Wars, with men away fighting, 'loggerettes' began working in the woods and the sawmills, taking over traditionally male tasks. While many enjoyed the work, most were asked to move aside once the men returned, reverting to their roles as homemakers and mothers.

'Loggerettes' worked in the woods during the World Wars.

INDIGENOUS LUMBERJACKS

Native peoples have always had a strong connection to the land, and many are striving to be responsible stewards of the forests today

Before Europeans arrived to colonise the 'New World', Native populations who had lived there for thousands of years already harvested trees for canoes, shelter, weapons and art, and used bark for food, medicine and baskets.

Indigenous peoples were forced to move onto farming reservations after Congress passed the Indian Appropriations Act in 1851, completely altering their way of life and restricting their ability to hunt, fish and gather their traditional foods. Conditions on the reservations were harsh and by the end of the 19th century, some Native Americans were working in the logging industry, travelling to find work and sending their wages back to their families on the reservations, or having their families join them. Many became team leaders thanks to their understanding of land management and natural instinct for forest work.

SAVVY STEWARDSHIP

Some communities, like the Menominee Indians of Wisconsin, began logging on their reservations. At first, the Menominee cut timber for their own use, but were later given permission to sell to outside sawmills, using the Wolf River for transportation. Between 1870 and 1890, the Indian lumberjacks cut and sold more than 88 million board feet of timber. They started a full-scale logging business, which drew in four million dollars around 1908, and opened their own sawmill in 1909.

Practising sustainable forestry, the Menominee people have maintained a healthy forest for over 150 years, and they're still logging today. In 1994, the Menominee became the first forest management enterprise in the United States to be certified by the Forest Stewardship Council (FSC).

VALUE OF NATURE

Other Native populations including the Klamath, Warm Springs, Siletz, Coquille, Grand Ronde and Umatilla of Oregon are also using sustainable logging methods, restoring the diversity of flora and fauna in large areas of their tribal forests. In Canada, First Nations people such as the Tl'azt'en Nation of British Columbia are striving to reconcile the benefit of commercial forestry operations with traditional indigenous values and preserve their lands through sustainable practices for years to come.

Logging camp on the Menominee Indian reservation, Wisconsin, US.

ON THE SKIDS

When it comes to the lumberjack dictionary, loggers left us more than 'Timber!' and 'Yo-ho!'

A 'skid road' at a lumber camp near Wilkeson, Washington, US, 1893.

The term 'skid row', meaning a poor city neighbourhood, became popular in America during the 1930s Great Depression, but did you know that its roots lie in the logging industry?

A 'skid road' was a route used to slide felled logs down to the river or a landing place, before they were transported to the mill. A street in Seattle, Washington, became the original urban skid road in the 1850s. Logs felled in the surrounding forests were greased and 'skidded' down a steep hill that led straight to the lumber mill, located on the Elliott Bay waterfront. Now known as Yesler Way, after the mill's founder, the street runs through the Pioneer Square-Skid Road Historic District, known for its food, arts and culture.

GRITTY CITY

In Canada, Vancouver had its own notorious skid road in what's now known as the city's Downtown Eastside. Both roads became hubs for men looking for work, and places to booze, brawl and flop when the labouring was done. During the dark days of the Depression, with no work to be found, destitute men would still gather along these roads, with the colloquial street names and their significance morphing into the term 'skid row'.

Many cities still have a gritty skid row district. Portland's Old Town Chinatown, downtown Los Angeles, Kensington in Philadelphia and San Francisco's Tenderloin District are some of the best known, while New York's Bowery was considered its skid row, before the regeneration of Manhattan.

Back in the forests, today's loggers are still skidding: pulling cut trees out of the forest on powerful skidders, before loading them onto trucks and transporting them to the mill.

HIP SKIDS

Skid Row was an early name used by Washington band Nirvana and is also the name of a rock band from New Jersey.

CHOPPING CHAMPIONSHIPS

Traditional logging activities inspired the international timbersports competitions and events that modern-day lumberjacks and Jills compete in today.
Here are the ones to watch

STIHL TIMBERSPORTS SERIES

Founded in 1985, this international series sees professional athletes, teams and rookies compete in extreme woodchopping disciplines using axes, saws and chainsaws. Men compete in six disciplines and women compete in three.

LUMBERJACK WORLD CHAMPIONSHIPS

This event has been drawing the world's greatest lumberjacks and Jills to Hayward, Wisconsin, every year since 1960 and includes 21 sawing, chopping, climbing and log-rolling competitions, plus three team contests.

SQUAMISH DAYS LOGGERS SPORTS FESTIVAL

Hosted annually in Squamish, British Columbia, this festival tests lumberjacks and Jills with a range of loggers sports, including chopping and sawing, log rolling, axe throwing and tree topping.

SYDNEY ROYAL EASTER SHOW

First held in 1823, this annual celebration of Australian culture includes the Woodchopping & Sawing Competition which sees athletes compete in underhand, standing block, tree felling, sawing and chainsaw events.

NEW YORK STATE WOODSMEN'S FIELD DAYS

Held each year in Boonville, New York, this homage to the lumberjack includes chopping and sawing events, along with axe throwing and log rolling.

JOHNNY APPLESEED FESTIVAL

Held annually in Sheffield, Pennsylvania, some of the world's best lumberjacks and Jills gather here to compete in chopping, sawing and axe-throwing events.

WEBSTER COUNTY WOODCHOPPING FESTIVAL

Top choppers have been competing for the Southeastern US World Championship Woodchopper title in Webster, West Virginia, every year since 1960.

FRYEBURG FAIR

Maine's largest agricultural fair started with humble beginnings in 1851 and today draws 225,000 spectators to watch athletes compete in 27 timbersports, including chopping, sawing, axe throwing and log rolling.

A man competes in a log-chopping contest, Lumbermen's Picnic, Canada, 1947.

FELLING FASHION

The classic plaid shirt has been in style for more than 170 years, with each generation adopting the flannel for its own. We follow the evolution of the lumberjack look

The Buffalo shirt has been a worldwide wardrobe staple since it was first woven by Woolrich in 1850. Like Levi's, Dr Martens, biker jackets or trench coats, the plaid shirt's appeal is timeless, and has been adopted and reimagined from generation to generation, with each pinning its own particular meaning to its checked lapel.

With its distinctive blocks of colour and tartan-style woven patterns, plaid was conceived in Scotland, taking its name from the Gaelic word *plaide*: a heavy cloak or blanket used to keep the Highlanders warm in winter. The famous red and black shirt we know today was born in a wool mill in rural Pennsylvania. Established in 1830 by John Rich, the son of a weaver who migrated to America from Liverpool in the early 1800s, the Woolrich company supplied woollen goods, like socks and blankets, to farms and lumber camps, delivering them by a mule-drawn cart.

The plaid lumberjack shirt has become a timeless wardrobe staple.

BIRTH OF AN ICON

During its 'lumberjack era' from 1830 to 1900, Woolrich was the brand of choice for loggers, hunters and trappers, and in 1850, the mill manufactured its first Wool Buffalo Check Shirt, made from the signature Buffalo Plaid. 'The shirt quickly became the symbol of lumberjacks and outdoorsmen, and it's remained an icon for over 170 years,' says Andrea Canè, the company's creative director. 'The distinct red and black colour offered high outdoor visibility, and our wool was the most technical fabric of the time, crafted for maximum breathability and high performance.'

'Mountain made' and 'soft and supple, yet tough as iron', Woolrich's outdoor wear was durable but stylish. The company's coordinating ensemble of plaid hunting coat, breeches and cap, which became known as the 'Pennsylvania Tuxedo', was tough enough to withstand the winter weather, yet chic enough to feature in the prestigious fashion archive at New York's Metropolitan Museum of Art.

No. 220 Cap
No. 150 Coat
No. 1990 Breeches

No. 221 Cap
No. 545 Jacket
No. 1953 Breeches

No. 223 Cap
No. 258 Coat
No. 1988 Breeches

Woolrich Stag Hunting Coats

No. 150—Oxford with small Green and Red overplaid.

No. 153—Maroon and Black hunter's plaid.

No. 146—Forester's Green.

Woolrich Hunting Breeches

To Match Hunting Coats

No. 1953B—Maroon a n d B l a c k hunter's plaid.

No. 1953BX—Maroon a n d B!ack hunter's plaid, double knees.

No. 1943B—Maroon and B l a c k hunter's plaid, double seat and knees, zipper fly and legs.

No. 1990B—Oxford, small Green and Red overplaid.

No. 1972B—Dark Gray mixture.

No. 1966B—Forester's Green.

No. 1988B—Red and Black plaid.

No. 220 Cap
No. 126 Cruiser Coat
No. 1990 Breeches

No. 220 Cap
No. 518 Jacket
No. 1988 Breeches

Woolrich Hunting Caps

No. 220 Red leather Cap with cloth ear flaps.

No. 221 All-wool Hunter's Red and Black plaid, reversible, with ear flaps.

No. 222 Plain Red, all-wool, with ear flaps.

No. 223 Red and Black hunter's plaid, hat style, with ear flaps.

All Caps can be worn with above hunting suits, and are water-proofed.

The plaid hunting suits produced by Woolrich became known as the 'Pennsylvania Tuxedo'.

The Particular Outdoor Man

Fine Shirts

Buffalo or Plaid Shirts

Woolrich Light Weight Concealed Zipper Shirts

The '60' Line

Talon Fastener Shirt

Updated versions of the Tuxedo have been produced throughout Woolrich's history, along with variations on the Buffalo plaid shirts and jackets.

FROM FOREST TO URBAN JUNGLE

By the 1950s, the plaid shirt had weaved its way into popular culture, with Marlon Brando famously sporting a flannel in 1954 film *On the Waterfront*, while actors and style icons including Audrey Hepburn and Marilyn Monroe made plaid their own in tie-front shirts and trousers. Even the middle classes began to follow in the giant footsteps of lumberjack folklore hero Paul Bunyan, stepping out in workwear that forged an affiliation with the great outdoors, while living increasingly suburban lifestyles.

In the late 1950s, Pendleton Woollen Mills in the northwest made a blue plaid surf shirt, adopted by up-and-coming Californian band The Pendletones. The group continued to sport the shirts on their record covers throughout the 1960s, even after changing their name and finding fame as The Beach Boys. Plaid had arrived at America's West Coast – and is still enjoying its time in the sun. 'Outdoor and utilitarian clothing offers the perfect mix of durability, performance and comfort,' says Andrea. 'These design traits make wearers feel protected and prepared for anything.'

COME AS YOU ARE

The 1970s and 1980s saw everyone from hippies to preppies and punks to pop stars parading in plaid, demonstrating its enduring flexibility and wearability. From the Sex Pistols to Spandau Ballet, Bowie to Bananarama, plaid has stamped

ABOVE: This excerpt from a Woolrich catalogue showcases hunting clothing in Buffalo check, a pattern first woven in 1850. OPPOSITE: The shirts of the Outdoor Man.

an indelible mark on our culture and shaped some of music's most memorable and iconic looks. Each subculture has transformed the traditional simplicity of the design into something uniquely theirs. The shirt continued to be adopted by a diverse range of youth movements throughout the 1990s. West Coast rappers including NWA and Snoop Dogg embraced oversized flannels and classic American workwear by brands like Carhartt, Ben Davis and Dickies. In Los Angeles, the Mexican-American Chicano subculture refashioned the shirts, with men wearing them open over a T-shirt, fastening only the top button. The style is also worn by *chola* girls, a Latina subculture influenced by hip-hop, whose strong look made it into the mainstream and has been mined by stars from Gwen Stefani to Rihanna.

19

The early 1990s grunge scene that came out of Seattle took the plaid shirt from its logging roots in the Pacific Northwest and shot it into the stratosphere, with bands including Nirvana, Soundgarden, Alice in Chains and Pearl Jam layering flannels over long-sleeved T-shirts. Nirvana's Kurt Cobain emerged as the scene's poster boy, although his dishevelled style was born out of necessity. As a boy growing up in Washington state, Cobain was skinny and often cold, so layering helped on both counts. He was also poor for much of his life – wearing secondhand work shirts from charity shops wasn't a contrived look.

EMPEROR'S NEW CLOTHES

When fashion house Perry Ellis dragged the grunge style off the streets and onto the catwalk in its Spring 1993 collection – with models 'dressing down' in layered plaid silk shirts, raglan tees and skirts with thousand-dollar-plus price tags – the move backfired, and not just with the working-class grunge kids.

Production was scrapped, designer Marc Jacobs was fired, and when the grunge clothing collection was sent as a marketing stunt to Cobain – who never endorsed a commercial brand in his life – he and his wife Courtney Love reacted in line with the movement's anticonsumerist ethos. 'We burned it. We were punkers – we didn't like that kind of thing,' Love revealed in a later interview.

Marc Jacobs brought grunge back 25 years later under his own label, modelled by a new generation of fashionistas. In an interview with Elle, he said: 'We bought vintage flannel shirts for $2 on St Marks Place and remade them out of silk. Taking something banal or vulgar and elevating it to designer status was not new. We were not the first to do it, but people got offended. They were adamant: No, you're not supposed to do that. But really, it's still happening. It's the emperor's new clothes... Isn't that what fashion has always been?'

HIP, HIP TODAY

At the turn of the millennium, hipsters seized the plaid baton, ran with it into the 2010s and are still running – or rather riding with it – on their fixed-gear bikes. Perhaps more than any other subculture's adoption of the plaid shirt, the hipster scene that emerged in the early 2000s in Brooklyn full-on embraced its logging history: beards, boots, beanies and all. Drawing on the bohemian hipster movement of the 1940s, the entrepreneurial, mainly middle-class, hip kids of Brooklyn – and soon after, London – embraced vintage clothes, retro authors and alternative music, blending ironic nerdiness with cultivated cool.

Today, the hipster and metrosexual's hirsute lovechild – the lumbersexual – is found across the globe, from the coffee bars of Melbourne's Fitzroy to the microbreweries of Anchorage, Alaska. They may not be sharpening their axes to build their own cabin or log rolling their way down the river to pick up their morning cup of flat white. They might prefer hitting up hip bars than wrangling in rough 'n' ready saloons. They may just like the look and feel of a casual plaid shirt and prefer the ease of growing a robust bush of facial hair. But whatever inspires them, the new generation of Buffalo-check bearers embodies the ideal of a simpler time, a connection to the natural world, and respect for authentic, hardworking lives well lived.

'The classic lumberjack shirt has really cemented itself in the fashion dialogue through its various adaptations in movies, music and subcultures,' says Andrea. 'From grunge to hipsters, the aesthetic has been used by very different communities that can each relate to its unique, durable, sustainable and non-conformist characteristics.'

Like the forests where it was first put to work, the black and red plaid shirt – and the spirit it represents – is evergreen.

Grunge bands like Nirvana made the plaid flannel shirt their own in the 1990s.

WOODCHOPPING WHISKERS

If you're truly embracing the lumberjack lifestyle, there's one accessory you can't be without: a lustrous bird-nest-sized beard

While the loggers of yore likely couldn't give a hairy monkey about sporting a stylish beard, the modern-day lumbersexual wouldn't be seen dead in the forest without some well-kept facial hair. Facial hair trends may have gone in and out of fashion, but the beard's raison d'être has endured since prehistoric man was out roaming the land with a club.

Firstly, beards help keep you warm in winter – just what you need for a day out felling in the snow – while even a little fuzz will shield your face from the sun in warmer months, too. Secondly, they protect your face and will cushion any blows heading your way from a falling branch – or even a flying fist. Many believe having a beard keeps you healthy,

trapping airborne toxins before they enter your mouth or nostrils. But most importantly, how much manlier does everyone look with some face foliage? Grow a beard and you're no longer one of the smooth-shorn sheep in the herd: you, my friend, are a courageous, testosterone-fuelled, mane-framed lion.

But whether you're rocking Hagrid-level hirsuteness or trying to tease the teeniest of beards from your bumfluff, these top grooming tips from the experts at the Lumberjack Beard Co. will help you to cultivate winning woodchopping whiskers.

A robust beard has become an essential feature of the lumberjack look.

Clean-shaven lumberjacks stand in front of a sequoia tree at Converse Basin, located in California, US.

LATHER LOVER

There are a few simple steps you can follow for a healthy, well-maintained lumberjack beard… and it all starts with cleanliness. An all-natural beard shampoo is a must. Regular varieties contain chemicals that lengthen their shelf life, but using these products will actually do more damage than good, leaving your beard dry and brittle. This is why you'll see so many beard-specific shampoos and co-washes on the market. The absence of additional chemicals in natural shampoos helps to preserve natural oils, thereby retaining moisture in your beard so that it doesn't dry out and become unmanageable. Lather up your beard with a natural shampoo, then rinse it out.

OIL IT UP

Once you've washed your beard with a natural shampoo, dab it with a towel to dry. Be careful not to rub it, as this could damage the hair at the roots. Then, before completely dry, you'll want to apply some beard oil. How much you use will depend on its length. For up to 2cm (1in) long, four to six drops will be enough. If 15cm (6in) or longer, you'll be looking to use between half to a full dropper's worth, to ensure the moisture from the oil reaches the tips of the hair. Squeeze the oil into your palm, then, with your fingers slightly apart, rub your palms together to spread it evenly between them. Next, brush your palms up through your beard, so that the oil reaches the skin underneath, before brushing them down the length of your beard, covering each hair with oil in the process. Finally, with a wide-toothed comb, smooth your beard into place. This will help spread the oil throughout.

> **DID YOU KNOW?**
> A healthy lifestyle can help to promote hair growth. Regular exercise, reducing stress levels, getting plenty of sleep and eating a balanced diet will boost your beard-growing potential.

HYDRATION STATION

Healthy skin equals a healthy beard, so the main purpose of the oil is to protect and hydrate the skin beneath the hair. You only need to apply beard oil once daily, first thing in the morning, to ensure both skin and beard are well hydrated for the day ahead. For those who like to shower in the evening, you'll need to apply more beard oil afterwards. Following these two steps alone will ensure your facial hair is healthy, full and well nourished: the most important part of beard maintenance.

BUTTER FINGERS

Once you've applied your oil, wait for at least five minutes before applying your beard balm or butter. This will allow time for the oil to work its way well into the hairs and skin beneath. While beard butter can be used at any time of the day, its nourishing qualities can add much-needed moisture to your beard throughout the night. Balm on the other hand is hardier and more robust, and is more commonly used to offer protection against the elements. Both are applied the same way. Scrape out roughly a thumbnail-sized amount of either onto your palm. With your fingers spread slightly apart, rub your palms together until the product becomes more liquid, then apply it to your beard. Balms will take longer to emulsify than butters because of the

BEARDY LIKE BUNYAN

The lumberjack aesthetic you know and love today comes from depictions of the legendary logger Paul Bunyan, who was portrayed as a big, burly man with a beard. A typical lumberjack from the late 1800s would have been around 1.7m (5ft 6in) tall, and was often clean-shaven. Beards attracted lice, which could be a problem in the logging camps, so big whiskers were a no-no.

higher concentration of beeswax or other holding agents used to make them. When your palms are thoroughly covered, run your fingers up through your beard, before running your palms down the length of your beard to create that protective shield.

BLOW YOUR BRISTLES

For a more stylised beard, use the cold setting on a hairdryer to set it. Hold the device about 15cm (6in) from your face, making sure to point the nozzle down the length of your beard only. Use a comb or brush to smooth your beard hair into place, straightening out any unruly curls in the process. The cold air will help to set the beeswax, giving you a neat, well-groomed look. You'll need to trim it occasionally to keep it in tip-top shape, so invest in a good pair of beard scissors, plus a beard-shaping tool to help with any tricky curves and angles. Now off a-lumbering you go.

Tools to take care of the beard. Wax, comb, brush and balm.

HOW TO
BE A WORLD
CHAMPION
LUMBERJACK

The Stihl Timbersports series sees some of the world's best athletes go head-to-head in extreme wood-cutting competitions. Current world champion Brayden Meyer reveals what it takes to be the ultimate lumberjack

Woodchopping has come a long way since the first competition between two axemen in Ulverstone, Tasmania in 1870. Betting $50 on who could chop 91cm (3ft) standing blocks the fastest, Joseph Smith and Jack Briggs unknowingly sparked what has become a 150-year-old timbersports tradition.

Competitive woodchopping was formally recognised in 1891, with the establishment of the United Australasian Axeman's Association and the inaugural Woodchopping World Championship, held at Atkinson's saleyards in Latrobe, Australia. The winner was Tom Reeves of Barrington, who chopped through a 61cm (2ft) standing block in 6 minutes, 22.5 seconds. The Australian Axeman's Hall of Fame and Timberworks marks the spot today. The first true World Championship Series was staged in Ulverstone in 1970, drawing teams from Australia, New Zealand, Canada and the United States, won by Tasmania's George Foster.

Australia is still leading the woodchopping charge today, with Victoria's Brayden Meyer holding the World Championship title in the men's division, and Australia's 'Chopperoos' holding the title in the team division of the Stihl Timbersports Series.

EXTREME ATHLETES

Stihl Timbersports began in 1985, with the earliest events broadcast from a field in Wisconsin – historically, one of the most prolific lumber-producing states in the US. Today, the series has a massive

Brayden cuts a 'cookie' at the Stihl Timbersports World Championship 2019.

global following and is broadcast on TV networks around the world, attracting top athletes to take part in regional, national and international competitions, with their roots deeply entwined in logging tradition. Andreas Stihl invented the first modern electric chainsaw in 1926, signalling the move away from human-powered axes and crosscut saws, but all three feature in the series.

The men's professional division features six disciplines: three with an axe (underhand chop, springboard and standing block chop) and three with

saws – single buck (using a crosscut saw), stock saw (using a heavy-duty chainsaw) and hot saw (a free class using customised chainsaws). The women's professional division includes three disciplines: the underhand chop, single buck and stock saw.

The winner is the athlete or team that collects the most points over the course of the competition. There are also rookie, intermediate and team divisions, and a challenging Champion's Trophy, where athletes complete four disciplines (underhand chop, single buck, standing block chop and stock saw), back-to-back.

Each discipline tests the endurance, strength and technical ability of the athletes against the clock, with the world's best woodcutters obliterating logs (from sustainably grown trees) in seconds, setting new world records faster than you can, er, swing an axe.

FAMILY TREE

Reigning world champion Brayden stormed away with the title at the 2019 Championships in Prague, Czech Republic, three years after becoming the Champion's Trophy holder in 2016. A fourth-generation woodchopper from Broadford, Australia, Brayden has timbersports in his blood and, when he's not competing around the world, works as a logger in the eucalyptus forests of Victoria's Central Highlands. 'My dad and uncles are all axemen, and I've grown up working with wood and handling chainsaws and axes,' says Brayden. 'I entered my first local woodchopping competition aged nine, but I've had an axe in my hand pretty much since I could walk.'

ABOVE: Brayden competes in the springboard competition at the Stihl Timbersports World Championship 2019 in Prague, Czech Republic. OPPOSITE: A competitor in a woodchopping event at the Gawler Show, South Australia, 1941.

Brayden was introduced to the Stihl Timbersports series by his uncle, Brad Turner, who's also a champion athlete. Brayden won his first national title in 2015, aged only 19 – the same year he took bronze in the World Championships. Along with his individual titles, he's also a five-time team world champion, thanks to wins with the Australian Chopperoos, and holds the current world record in the underhand chop event with a time of just 12.39 seconds.

Now 26, Brayden is at the top of his game, winning the Australian virtual championships in 2020. At 1.9m (6ft, 2in) and weighing in at an impressive 120kg (265lb), he's a force to be reckoned with, combining incredible strength with stamina and agility.

'My job is very physical, which definitely helps with my fitness, but I also do a lot of running and cycling. Repetition is the best training, so I do two sessions of two or three hours every week, where I practise the timbersports disciplines,' he says. 'I've always believed that if you work hard at something, you'll see the results and earn the rewards.'

HOW TO BE THE BEST

Brayden says: 'Aim to strike the block at 45-degree angles and don't hold the axe too close to your body. Old timers say "aim for the grass" for your up hits and "reach for the sky" for the down hits. Put everything you've got into your swing, develop a rhythm and focus on the point you want to hit or you'll miss it.'

UNDERHAND CHOP

The athlete stands on top of a horizontally mounted 61m (2ft) long tree trunk, which measures just over 30cm (1ft) in diameter. At the starting signal, they must chop through the log from both sides with their axe, cutting the log completely in two as fast as they can. Steel mesh socks to protect the feet and shins are a must.

WORLD RECORD HOLDER

Australia's Brayden Meyer chopped his way into the record books with a time of just 12.39 seconds at the 2015 event in Poznan, Poland. Australia's Amanda Beans holds the women's world record, with a time of 36.16 seconds, set at the 2019 Australian World Championships.

WHAT'S THE HISTORY?

This replicates bucking felled trees into manageable logs, before they were hauled from the forest to the mill.

Get to know six extreme timbersports and Brayden's tips for smashing them:

STANDING BLOCK CHOP

Competitors must use their axe to chop through both sides of a block of wood in the fastest time. The timber measures around 30cm (1ft) in diameter and is anchored vertically in a metal stand.

WORLD RECORD HOLDER

The United States' Matt Cogar shattered the record at the 2018 event in Liverpool, with a time of 11.03 seconds.

WHAT'S THE HISTORY?

This discipline closely simulates the action of felling a tree. It requires powerful, fast and accurate strikes with the axe.

HOW TO BE THE BEST

Brayden says: 'Most people start off doing the underhand chop, as it's one of the safest timbersports disciplines. Focus on honing your timing and hand-eye coordination. Once you've nailed your technique, it's about making sure you have the stamina to keep going.'

SPRINGBOARD

At the starting signal, competitors use their axe to chop a 10cm (4in) deep pocket into a vertically mounted log at shoulder height. Slotting a wooden 'springboard' into the gap, they stand on it and chop a second shoulder-height pocket into the log, slotting another board into it. Standing on the second, 1.8m (6ft) above the ground, they must cut through a block of wood at the top of the log. The first to do it, wins.

WORLD RECORD HOLDER

Canada's Stirling Hart set the current record with a time of 35.67 seconds at the 2016 World Championships in Stuttgart, Germany.

WHAT'S THE HISTORY?

This technique was used by loggers to make cutting platforms, allowing them to chop above the hard root base or spur of a tree, which could be several feet tall.

HOW TO BE THE BEST

Brayden says: 'It's important to work on building up your leg strength and agility for this event, as you need to be quick jumping up onto the boards. Bike riding is a good way to get your legs in shape, but be sure to keep practising your chopping technique so you become faster, stronger and more accurate, too.'

RIGHT: Brayden takes on the underhand chop at 2019's Stihl Timbersports World Championship in Prague, Czech Republic.
OPPOSITE: JH Matheson competes in the tree felling competition at the Royal Adelaide Show at Wayville, South Australia, in 1948.

Brayden demonstrates his chainsaw skills during the hot saw competition at the 2019 Stihl Timbersports Championship in Prague, Czech Republic.

SINGLE BUCK

The athlete uses a 1.7m (5ft 8in) to 1.9m (6ft 4in) crosscut saw to cut a complete wooden disc or 'cookie' off a horizontally fixed, white-pine tree trunk, approximately 45cm (1.5ft) in diameter, in the shortest time possible. The competitor can spray the saw with oil before they start to help with lubricity.

WORLD RECORD HOLDER

Canadian Ben Cumberland sawed through a log in 12.94 seconds at the 2019 Prague World Championships.

New Zealand's Jason Wynyard set a record of 9.39 seconds at the 2007 US International Championships, which he held for 12 years before a rule change, which stopped assistants aiding athletes in the event. Germany's Svenja Bauer set a new women's world record (with assistant) of 16.83 seconds at the 2014 German Women Jungheinrich Cup.

WHAT'S THE HISTORY?

While the saws used in the competition are made for racing, they're based on the design of the 'misery whip': the traditional two-man crosscut saw, once widely used for cutting logs.

HOW TO BE THE BEST

Brayden says: 'Don't let the length of the saw put you off: this isn't as hard as it looks once you get the hang of it. Let the saw do the work, but use your legs, arms and hips to keep it moving and sawing freely.'

STOCK SAW

At the signal, competitors pick up the idling MS661 chainsaw and cut two cookies of a specified thickness from a marked area of a horizontally mounted poplar log. The fastest competitor to perform one downwards and one upwards cut on the 41cm (16in) diameter log wins.

WORLD RECORD HOLDER

Marcin Juskowski of Poland set a new record at the 2020 Polish Championships, with a time of 9.51 seconds.

Alrun Uebing from Moschheim in Germany holds the women's world record of 9.60 seconds, set at 2020's German Amarok Cup.

WHAT'S THE HISTORY?

This event demonstrates the chainsaw skills of the athlete – and requires the strength, accuracy and control shown by lumberjacks using these powerful tools in the forest.

HOW TO BE THE BEST

Brayden says: 'Using a chainsaw can be daunting at first, so take your time getting to know how it feels and works. Make sure you have a good grip on the handles and start sawing slowly, building your pace over time. This discipline is about speed, but also controlled and accurate cutting.'

HOT SAW

This is the finale of any Stihl event. Athletes must start the saw and cut three cookies of a specified thickness from a horizontally mounted tree trunk, approximately 46cm (1.5ft) in diameter, as quickly as possible. The first cut is downwards, followed by upwards, then downwards again. The powerful, custom-built chainsaws are made with 250–400cc (cubic centimetre) single-cylinder engines, taken from dirt bikes, jet skis or snowmobiles. They can weigh up to 30kg (66lb), have a chain speed of 250km/h (155mph) and are very loud.

WORLD RECORD HOLDER

Dirk Braun from Germany set the current record at the 2016 German National Championships, with a scorching time of just 5.2 seconds.

WHAT'S THE HISTORY?

The crowd's favourite event, and one of the most challenging for competitors, the hot saw competition draws on engineering skills, as well as chainsaw ability. Like the resourceful lumberjacks of the past, athletes modify their tools, or work with engineers, to get the maximum results.

HOW TO BE THE BEST

Brayden says: 'My saw comes from the US and it's custom-made with a 330cc engine. It weighs around 30kg (66lb), but once it's going, I don't really notice the weight. These saws aren't for beginners: they're a bit like having a powerful motorbike in your hand! Start using a regular chainsaw first and once you've mastered that and feel confident, move on to the hot saw.

'During the competition season there's usually a chopping event each weekend and I love it. I've been brought up with the sport, and it's a great community: we're competitive, but we support each other, too.'

TOOLS OF THE TRADE

Today's high-tech harvesters and forwarders can cut and clear trees with ease, but in the 1800s, logging with human-powered hand tools was back-breaking work. Here's a guide to the essential old-school lumberjack hardware

AXE

The essential and most iconic of all lumberjack accessories, the axe was the primary tool used for felling trees until saws became the preference in the 1880s. Loggers had the choice of two heads: single- or double-bitted, with many different head shapes and weights to choose from. Wider blades are better for chopping softwoods, and narrow blades are better for hardwoods. Axes were also used for cutting the branches off trees, known as 'limbing'.

CROSSCUT SAW

Still widely used around the world, one- or two-person crosscut saws – measuring from 1.2 to 4.9m (4–16ft) – are designed to cut across the wood grain. Felling saws for cutting down trees have a concave back, and are lighter and more flexible with a narrower blade; while bucking saws for cutting trees into logs have a straight back and are heavier and stiffer, with a broader blade. Loggers call the two-person saw the 'misery whip', reflecting the hardship of a day felling trees by hand in the forest.

BOW SAW

First developed in Sweden, the smaller, one-person bow saw – also known as a buck- or Swede saw – cuts smaller logs, less than 25cm (10in) in diameter. It was the tool of choice for cutting pulpwood – used for making paper products – in Canada and the US.

WEDGE

Essential for felling, bucking and splitting wood, wedges lift the tree, preventing it from sitting back when it's being felled. They also reduce binds on the saw during bucking,

TWICE AS TOUGH
On a double-bitted axe, one edge is usually sharp for chopping, and the other is 'stunt' or thicker for work where it may hit metal, stone or tree knots.

A logger uses a crosscut saw in Malheur National Forest, Oregon, US, 1942.

allowing the tool to continue to move freely. In the early 1800s, lumberjacks used old axe handles or wooden wedges to help fell a tree, with steel and iron varieties coming into play towards the end of the century. They usually measure up to 30cm (12in) and are 2cm (1in) thick at the head (splitting wedges are usually thicker and longer).

PEAVEY

This long pole (also called a stock or handle) has a metal spike or pick at the end and a lever to help grab and turn logs. Named after Joseph Peavey, the blacksmith who invented the tool that revolutionised the logging industry in 1857, the Peavey Manufacturing Company still makes them today.

CANT HOOK

Similar to a peavey but, instead of a point at the end, fitted with a metal

HOOKED ON THE RIVER

In the heyday of the river drives, Maine's Peavey Manufacturing Company made 12 different styles of hooks. The last Maine river drive was in 1976, when trains and trucks took over transporting logs to the mill.

thimble with a bill and a lever. Used more frequently at the landing in the forest or the mill – rather than on the river – its primary use is for rolling logs.

PIKE POLE

This wooden tool, with a straight metal spike and hook at the end, was used to transport logs along the river and construct timber rafts.

PULP HOOK

A short, one-handed device, used for moving small logs of pulpwood. The hook is made of steel with an oval handle and is useful for handling frozen wood.

CALK OR CAULK BOOTS

This tough, spike-soled footwear gave better traction when logging in damp forests, and riding the logs on rumbling rivers during the spring drive. The boots are still worn by forestry workers today.

BELOW: Two men use cant hooks to move a fallen tree at camp near Effie, Minnesota, US, 1937.
OPPOSITE: Two lumberjacks pose with the tools of their trade in Wisconsin, US, ca. 1900.

BUTT OR POLL
Blunt back of axe-head, helps with balance and control

HEAD
'Business end' of the axe, usually made from stainless or carbon steel, comes in many shapes and sizes

BELLY
Curve in the handle's upper section

CHEEK
Smooth section of each side of the head

SHOULDER
Sturdy region lying just below the butt or poll

WEDGE
Made of metal or wood, this helps to secure the head inside the eye

BEARD
Underside of the head between the handle and heel

BEVEL OR CHISEL
Angled, polished section near the bit that determines the angle of approach into the wood

EYE
Hole where the handle fits into the head

BIT OR EDGE
Sharp, cutting side of the head

TOE
Upper corner of the bit

HEEL
Bottom corner of the bit

KNOB OR BELL
Very end of the
axe handle

WEDGE ALERT
The phrase 'to fly off
the handle' – meaning to
lose emotional control –
came from the uncontrolled
way an axe head can fly
from its handle if it
isn't properly
wedged.

THROAT
Curved lower section
of the handle

HANDLE
Traditionally made from
hardwoods like ash or
hickory, some are crafted
from steel or durable
synthetic materials
including fibreglass

ANATOMY OF AN AXE

There's more to this tool than just a head and a handle –
many elements are named after body parts. Here's an in-depth
dissection of the lumberjack's trusty chopper

HOW TO
AXE THROW
LIKE A BOSS

Yo-ho! It's time to axe throw. And nobody is more qualified to help you hit the bullseye than seven-time world champion lumberjack Darren Hudson

No activity is better at hurling us back to our primordial roots than throwing an axe. One of the world's earliest known tools, teardrop-shaped axes dating back 1.8 million years have been excavated in Lake Turkana in northwest Kenya, while the first axe with a handle, found in northwestern Australia's Windjana Gorge, is up to 49,000 years old. An essential lumberjack tool, European versions were used by early loggers, but weightier designs were needed to quickly fell trees and clear lands, so blacksmiths began to counterweight the back of the axe head, increasing the cut on each stroke. The iconic US double-bitted axe reared its head around the time of the Civil War. Symmetrical with wide blades either side of the handle, this was the tool of legendary Paul Bunyan, with one bit often used for heavy work like splitting and the other finely honed for cutting.

Axe-throwing champion, seven-time log-rolling world champion and 12-time Canadian champion log-roller Darren Hudson is a fifth-generation lumberjack, who keeps up his family traditions logging pine and spruce on their land in Nova Scotia. A self-confessed axe maniac (in the best possible sense), Darren also runs Wild Axe Productions, which offers wannabe lumberjacks and Jills the chance to learn the skills of Nova Scotia's expert woodsmen in its Lumberjack AXEperience. He's also an in-demand axe designer, owner of The Timber Lounge axe-throwing bar in Moncton and has even created a pilsner called Wild Axe with local craft brewing company Boxing Rock.

'My family have been driving logs down the Barrington River since 1883,' he says. 'And I've been log rolling since I was in the womb, because my mother used to compete in lumberjack competitions before I was born. I first competed aged nine and was tall, skinny and fast, so was

Champion lumberjack Darren wields his custom-designed Wild Axe Dragon.

good at tree climbing and log rolling. But the beauty of axe throwing is that you can still do it in the twilight of your career – well into your eighties if your shoulders hold up – because it requires flexibility and coordination, rather than strength.'

Tempted? Here are Darren's six tips to becoming an axe aficionado:

1. 'There's more than one good way to throw an axe and as we're all built differently, everybody will have their own style. You'll discover what works best for you the more you practise.'

2. 'Always make sure the area is clear of people before throwing.'

3. 'Square up to the target and plant your feet firmly on the ground, shoulder-width apart with your best foot slightly forward, which will help you to feel balanced. Using two hands is easier for beginners. Stand behind the throwing line and position yourself directly in line with the bullseye. If you'd rather use one hand, you'll need to line up the shoulder of your throwing arm instead.'

4. 'It helps to have a good eye, so make sure you stay focused on the bullseye at the centre of the target during your throw.'

5. 'Try not to hold the handle too hard, as this makes it harder to let go and keep it on target. If you're using two hands, bring the axe directly back over your head, like you're throwing a ball. Then power forward with your body, swinging your axe overhead. Fully extend your arms and release when your hands are pointed at the bullseye. To use one hand, bring the axe back past your ear until it nearly touches your shoulder, keeping it straight. Then bring your arm forward and release when the handle is vertical in front of you. A clean and consistent release is the key to success.'

6. 'Work on your body's flexibility to ensure you have the proper range of motion to maintain balance throughout your throw. And most of all, enjoy it!'

HOW DO I GET STARTED?

For your first foray into axe throwing, go to a facility where a professional will show you the ropes, they have good safety standards in place and you can use their axes. The sharper the tool, the safer it will be, as it's more likely to stick in the target. If you take it further, you'll need a special axe for throwing, rather than a general one from a hardware store, choosing one that's right for your build. Find out more, and how to make your own axe, in the next section.

LEFT: Darren continues the lumberjack legacy that his uncle and fellow axeman Stanley Scott started. **OPPOSITE:** Coaches at the Timber Lounge in Moncton, New Brunswick, Canada demonstrate how to throw an axe.

THE COMPETITION

Competitors must stand behind the throwing line and throw their axe at a wooden target, 6.1m (20ft) away. If a thrower steps over the line before or during their throw, they score zero. The target consists of rings worth 1–5 points, scoring higher the closer your axe lands to the bullseye. Only the fore-bit of the double-bit axe can score a hit, and it must stick into the target area. The fore-bit only needs to touch the line separating two scoring areas to win the higher points. The winner is whoever has the best score after three goes, although playing the best of five or six throws is also common.

SINGLE-BIT AXE HEADS

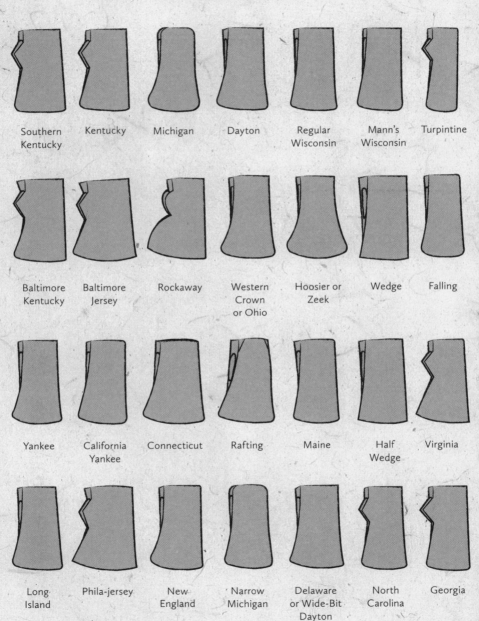

Southern Kentucky   Kentucky   Michigan   Dayton   Regular Wisconsin   Mann's Wisconsin   Turpintine

Baltimore Kentucky   Baltimore Jersey   Rockaway   Western Crown or Ohio   Hoosier or Zeek   Wedge   Falling

Yankee   California Yankee   Connecticut   Rafting   Maine   Half Wedge   Virginia

Long Island   Phila-jersey   New England   Narrow Michigan   Delaware or Wide-Bit Dayton   North Carolina   Georgia

DOUBLE-BIT AXE HEADS

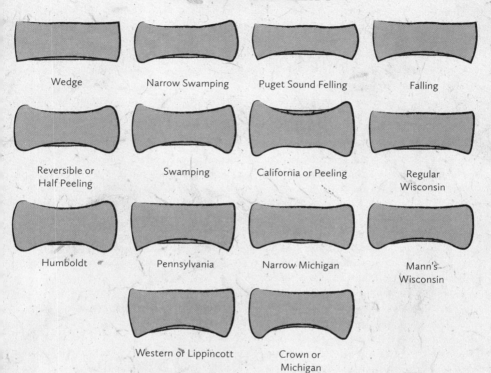

Wedge

Narrow Swamping

Puget Sound Felling

Falling

Reversible or
Half Peeling

Swamping

California or Peeling

Regular
Wisconsin

Humboldt

Pennsylvania

Narrow Michigan

Mann's
Wisconsin

Western or Lippincott

Crown or
Michigan

HEADS UP!

Axe heads come in many
different shapes and sizes,
with patterns often named
for the region where they
were first used

MAKE AN AXE

Humans have been using them for millennia, but how do you forge an axe of champions? Legendary blacksmith Hayward Meisner shares his expert tips for transforming metal into something magic

The essential lumberjack's tool needs to be as strong as the person wielding it, and making a great axe takes skill, patience and passion. Blacksmith Hayward Meisner has all these qualities in spades, producing ornamental ironwork and traditionally crafted axes from his ironworks forge in Lockeport, Nova Scotia, Canada.

Hayward was first introduced to metalworking by a friend who was visiting the region for the summer. 'I tried it, and from the moment I started working with metal, I was completely hooked,' says Hayward. So much so, that he switched careers from electrician to blacksmith, building and equipping his own forge and shop 40 years ago. Working with both traditional and modern tools, Hayward is helping to keep historic crafts alive, while inspiring a younger generation of local blacksmiths to take up the trade at the same time.

'It's a privilege to work with tools that haven't changed for generations,' he says. 'Like the anvil, the axe is a perfectly designed implement with so many uses. I'll never tire of forging a good axe.'

Hayward demonstrates how to forge an axe:

1. 'First, you need to decide on the weight and choose your steel accordingly. For a 1.6kg (3.5lb) axe, you'll need around 1.7kg (3.75lb) of carbon steel – the carbon ensures the axe will be hard. Next, holding the steel in a vice, mark a hole where the eye of the axe will sit – this is important for the symmetry of your tool. I'm making a double-bit, so the eye will sit in the centre. For a single-bit axe, the eye will be closer to the butt.'

2. 'Now heat the steel block in the forge, using iron tongs. Working with steel requires extreme heat. For me, a good forging temperature is between 538–982°C (1,000–1,800°F), after which the steel will melt. Coal is used traditionally, which turns to "coke" when it's burned on a fire, releasing the intensity of heat you'll need to work with the metal.'

3. 'Holding the steel with tongs, use a sharp punch to cut through the metal and make the eye. This is done from both sides, so the hole meets in the middle.'

4. 'Use a drift (a tapered metal rod) to widen the eye until it's big enough to accommodate the handle, carefully knocking it through the steel with a mallet. This doesn't remove any steel but moves it so the sides of the block will bulge a little.'

5. 'Turning the block on its side, use a hammer to correct the alignment of the steel, before doing the same on the other side, working both sides equally. At this stage, the steel is like putty or clay, but if it gets too cold, it will no longer be malleable.'

LOOK SHARP
It's important to sharpen your axe with a slow-turning grinding wheel, as a fast-turning belt could heat up the steel enough to affect the tempering of the blade.

6. 'Next, it's time to fan the blade, hammering it and pushing the steel to form the shape of your axe head, ensuring both bits are symmetrical if you're making a double-bit axe.'

7. 'Now your axe is really starting to take shape. Once the steel changes colour from yellow to cherry red it's starting to cool down, although it's still extremely hot.'

ARM'S LENGTH
The length of handle on your axe should measure roughly the same length as your arm, from the fingertips to the top.

too hard to be brittle and break, or so soft that the blade edge will bend over or mash. As you run the flame over the metal, you'll see the colour change from straw to purple, to blue, and then to deep blue, which means it's at the optimum temperature for tempering. If you see grey, you've heated the steel too much.'

8. 'It's time to quench the axe using water or oil. A red-hot piece of steel plunged into water will quickly make the water boil away from the metal, so the steel will take longer to cool. Oil doesn't heat up as quickly, so it cools the metal faster. Quenching leads to hardening of the metal, which makes it too brittle to work with, so the metal needs to be tempered.

'Tempering uses a more controllable heat source, like a propane flame. This important process resoftens the metal just the right amount, so it's no longer

9. 'Once tempered, the axe head should have a heat bath for around an hour at 200°C (400°F) – a nice spa treatment – which allows the molecules to settle into position. Then the handle is inserted and fixed in the eye with a wedge. This Dragon Axe, designed by champion axe thrower Darren Hudson, is marked with scallop shapes made on a die grinder, so it's as beautiful to look at as it is to use.'

LEFT: Hayward at work in his forge.
ABOVE: The world's largest axe is in Nackawic, a former Forestry Capital of Canada. Made from 50 tonnes (55 tons) of stainless steel, the base serves as an events stage, while a time capsule is embedded in the 7m-long (23ft) axe-head.

THE LEGENDARY LOGGER
PAUL BUNYAN

Born from forest folklore, larger-than-life lumberjack
Paul Bunyan and his companion, Babe the Blue Ox,
have become icons of American culture

Even if you've never heard of the world's most famous lumberjack, Paul Bunyan, you've probably seen him. The giant axeman has popped up in films such as the Coen brothers' *Fargo*, welcoming visitors entering the town of Brainerd, and Andrés Muschietti's big-screen adaptation of Stephen King's novel It, when a statue of the logger wielding a giant peavey comes to life in Derry in *Chapter Two*. Bunyan also stars in the less terrifying animated eponymous musical by Walt Disney. And if you're ever road-tripped around America, you'll have likely driven past him a few times, too.

The original statue that influenced King's book can be found in Bangor, Maine. Made of steel and fibreglass and standing over 9.1m (30ft) tall, it was erected in 1959 and is believed to be the largest statue of Bunyan in the world. Many others exist, the super-sized, plaid-shirt-wearing woodsman looming large in towns across the US, from Bemidji, Minnesota (home to the oldest

statue, dating from 1937) to Klamath in California, where a 15m (49ft) animatronic version waves his hand at visitors to the Trees of Mystery nature attraction, with a booming: 'Hello there!'

MAN OR MYTH?

But how did the legend of the towering tree cutter grow to such epic proportions? Tall tales featuring bumper-sized Bunyan and his equally brawny blue ox, Babe, first emerged in North America's early logging camps. According to *Out of the Northwoods: The Many Lives of Paul Bunyan* by author Michael Edmonds, the earliest reliable account was from a lumber camp in Wisconsin in the winter of 1885–1886. As workers moved from season to season and state to state, the tales they told moved with them, becoming bigger and bolder with each retelling.

A giant 9.4m (31ft) tall Paul Bunyan statue greets visitors to Bangor, Maine, US.

PAUL BUNYAN DAY
So famous is the lumbering logger, that he even has his own special day – 28 June. If there's ever a time to cook up some pancakes or throw an axe, this is it.

The Paul Bunyan and Babe the Blue Ox statues in Klamath, California, US are visible from Highway 101.

While some believe the legend of Bunyan could be based on a real-life lofty lumberjack – both Bangor in Maine and Bemidji in Minnesota claim to be his birthplace, and there are records of woodsmen recounting first-hand encounters with Paul and his crew – the stories of his superhuman size and endeavours place him firmly in the fictional realm. Even the burliest of shanty boys would have struggled to carve the Grand Canyon with their axe, dig out the Great Lakes as watering troughs for Babe or create 10,000 lakes from their footprints as they strode around Minnesota chasing a big, blue ox.

Bunyan allegedly created the Mississippi River, when a water tank he was pulling developed a leak, and tales of Paul's birth were pretty epic, too. It took five giant storks to deliver him as a baby, he could fit into his father's clothes at one week old and the family needed 10 cows to supply enough milk to keep him happy. He ate 40 bowls of oatmeal a day

and once, by rolling over, he caused an earthquake. The woods were the safest place for the rapidly growing boy, and here he felled trees at superhuman speed and developed a passion for pancakes, or flapjacks, cooked on a vast griddle in a gargantuan kitchen.

OUT OF THE WOODS

Reference to the logging legend first made it into print in 1893, when 'Paul Bunion' was mentioned in Michigan's *Gladwin County Record*, while Minnesota's *Duluth News Tribune* was the first to publish a story about the lumberjack in an article entitled 'Caught on the Run' in 1904. With news of the woodsman's incredible antics spreading, *Outer's Book* magazine ran an article featuring three Bunyan tales, called 'Some Lumberjack Myths', in 1910. Written by James Rockwell and reprinted in *The Washington Post*, its popularity led to Rockwell writing 16 more stories about Paul and his ox, who was allegedly blue due to North Dakota's notorious 'winter of the blue snow' – a treacherous cold snap that struck in 1886–1887. Also in 1910, reporter James MacGillivray's story 'The Round River Drive' was published in the *Detroit News Tribune*, which told tales from *Legends of Paul Bunyan, Lumberjack* by K Bernice Stewart and Homer A Watt, published in 1916 – the first scholarly collection of stories that had been circulating around the logging camps for 30 years or more. Through interviews with lumber workers, the authors drew together anecdotes from a range of states, including Wisconsin, Michigan, Minnesota, Washington and Oregon. Describing him as 'a powerful giant, seven feet tall and with a stride of seven feet,' they confirmed that 'he was famous throughout the lumbering districts for his great physical strength' but deemed some of the loggers' yarns 'too coarse for publication'.

HIT THE ROAD

Minnesotans are mad for all things Bunyan. The state's Paul Bunyan Scenic Byway is a 87km (54 mile) scenic route encompassing hiking and walking trails, beaches, parks and gardens. Meanwhile, the 193km (120 mile) Paul Bunyan Trail is Minnesota's longest biking trail.

qualities, while his blue ox was christened Babe. Pictured for the first time, Red River trademarked Laughead's illustration of Bunyan's head and began to use his name in business dealings.

Now with broader appeal, this marketable version epitomised the big, burly, hardworking woodcutter, complete with check shirt, beard and a double-bit axe: the classic lumberjack image was born.

Featured in hundreds of books for both children and adults, and inspiring songs, cartoons, poems and even an eponymous operetta – written by Anglo-American poet W H Auden and British composer Benjamin Britten and premiered in New York in 1941 – the legendary lumberjack's tales have not only endured but are also endlessly evolving, woven as firmly into the fabric of American folklore as Bunyan's Buffalo plaid shirt.

INTO THE SPOTLIGHT

The Red River Lumber Company of Minneapolis seized on the character's growing popularity and began publishing promotional brochures featuring Bunyan in 1914 – the first entitled *Introducing Mr Paul Bunyan of Westwood, California*. In the hands of Minnesotan copywriter William B Laughead, who went on to produce *Tales about Paul Bunyan, Vol. II* and *The Marvelous Exploits of Paul Bunyan*, the woodsman became imbued with increasingly superhuman

MUFFLER MAN

A giant statue of Bunyan was erected in 1962 to promote the Paul Bunyan Cafe on Route 66 in Flagstaff, Arizona. Produced by Bob Prewitt, founder of the Californian International Fiberglass company, this was the first of hundreds of giant 'muffler men' built in the next decade, used to advertise stores, goods and services across the United States and Canada.

A LUMBERJACK'S TALE

Freezing winters, soaking-wet socks and pilfering raccoons –
take a journey down the Barrington River in Canada's
Nova Scotia with Stanley Scott, 88, who recalls what
life was like as a lumberjack in the 1940s

Biting cold and roaring, the river was raging over rocks, forming rapids in its path – rapids that now held me firmly in their icy grip. Seconds before, I'd been riding a log, guiding others alongside me over the rocks – until one rolled into me, knocking me into the freezing water and pinning me up to my neck. I thought I was a goner for sure...

As the 'river boss', I knew the dangers of the springtime log drive, when crews of men would guide the felled trees along the Barrington River, down from the logging camps to my family's sawmill in Shelburne County. Jams would sometimes form along the way, with logs backing up on the bends or hitching on hidden rocks. The men often had to free up the logs. Some crews would use dynamite if the jam was too tight, but we had some pretty good drivers who could oust them with their peaveys alone: I was one of them. Displacing the logs was a dangerous job.

After dislodging the obstruction, the whole works would start moving – with you on it! It was easy to fall in or for your legs to get trapped. I had to rescue plenty of fellas from the water, but luckily that day one of them was looking out for me. Seeing me in trouble, he ferried a log across the river, rolled away the one that had me trapped and pulled me out. We had a solid crew, and our strong sense of camaraderie saved many lives.

INTO THE WOODS

My great-grandfather started our sawmill in 1883, and five generations of the family have been involved in the timber trade since. I've been at it myself for a long time, working in all areas of the business, from logging to river driving and sawing the logs at the mill, so I know my wood.

Stanley Scott at the Barrington River log drive, 1956.

Stanley and the crew keep the logs moving at Chrissy's Falls, from the Barrington River log drive, 1957.

Our 5,000 acres of land is covered with spruce, pine, hemlock and oak, and our timber has been used for building fishing boats.

I first went to help fell trees as a 12-year-old. Most logging took place in winter, when there was snow on the ground. We slept in a big tent in the woods, and cooked and ate our meals in another. Waking up for breakfast at 6 am, we'd be greeted by a large pot of oatmeal or cornmeal already cooking on the stove. We'd dip our bowl in, add a spoonful of molasses or sugar and eat our fill around the fire before heading into the forest with our crosscut saws and axes to start felling. Sometimes work would be in pairs, the fella with me notching the trees and driving the wedges in before I'd start sawing, and at other times it was a solo job. At 10 am we'd stop for a snack of bread, spread with molasses, and tea – there was no fresh milk or cream, so canned had to suffice. Again at noon we'd have the same, then fell trees all afternoon, finally finishing at around 6 pm. Food at camp was pretty good, with hearty meals

of salted foods or corned beef and pork, served with vegetables and potatoes. After dinner, there was always something to do, from mending our shoes, pike poles or peaveys, to telling yarns. Sometimes one of the crew would play a song on their mouth organ or fiddle to lift our spirits, and we'd all sing along.

Aged 14, I went on my first spring drive, helping to guide cut logs down the Barrington to the family sawmill. In my younger years, I was good at being a driver – going most days on a log, even riding them through the rapids. Still, it could be wet work – we'd camp in tents along the way and slept every night in damp clothes. I remember my boss telling us not to dry them too much at the end of each day or we'd catch a cold. Maybe he was right, because somehow we never got ill, despite our soaking socks doubling up as pillows!

Of course, there were wild animals out in the woods. One night, a black bear wandered into our camp and spooked our horse, which bolted for home, before we chased him off with our peaveys. The

Stanley and a fellow 'river hog' working on the Clyde River log drive, 1932.

raccoons were more troublesome. They're pretty smart but pesky too, and we'd often find them unscrewing the lids and dipping their paws into our jars of peanut butter.

A LUMBERJACK LEGACY

Some crews used horses to pull the chopped logs on sleds to the river, but we used a pair of oxen. Either method was better for the forest than today's machinery, which can wreck the land if not properly managed. The first time my uncle brought home a powered chainsaw, my father couldn't get to grips with it and thought it was dirty and loud, so ended up throwing it into the swamp! I fished it out, cleaned and repaired it, and slowly we all learned to use them.

My later years were spent driving skidders (heavy vehicles used to carry the wood to the river bank) and logging trucks, which eventually replaced the river drives. I was a licensed guide for a while, too. I worked with a naturalist who wrote for *Rod & Gun* magazine, which was about the outdoor life in Canada –

I believe some of his stories about our local deer inspired the classic Disney movie *Bambi*. I also competed in lumberjack sports – my favourites being log rolling and canoe racing. My nephew Darren has carried on the family tradition, becoming a seven-time world champion log roller and running the Wild Axe Lumberjack AXEperience, which offers visitors a chance to be a lumberjack for the day.

Our family has an 80-year-old logging camp, which we still use today, and I like to head over there for some quiet time with my dog Billy, a Nova Scotia Duck Tolling Retriever. I've had lots of interesting and exciting experiences, and I've loved living the life of a lumberjack. There's no doubt it's hard work, but it's healthy, too, and at 88, I still like to get out and spend time in the forest or work in the sawing mill.

We've always taken great care of our woods and still do, which is why we're able to make a good living over 130 years since we first logged our land. I hope that's the way things will continue for years and generations to come.

WWII LUMBERJILLS: THE FORGOTTEN ARMY

Not all World War II heroes fought on the frontline. In Great Britain, a hidden troop of women were waging their own daily battle in the forests, armed with axes and crosscut saws

Many valiant army divisions are remembered for the part they played in World War II, but there's one unit that slipped under the radar: the Women's Timber Corp (WTC). This forestry branch of the British Women's Land Army fulfilled a critical role during the war, yet until recently its contribution to the war effort has gone largely unnoticed.

Nicknamed the forgotten army, it consisted of 15,000 to 18,000 lumberjills who responded to the 1941 call from Ernest Bevin, the Minister for Labour and National Service, for women volunteers: 'One million wives were wanted for war work; inconvenience would have to be suffered and younger women would have to go where their services were required. It would be better to suffer temporarily than to be in perpetual slavery to the Nazis.'

The WTC was formed in 1942, after Germany's occupation of Norway cut off the transportation of essential wood supplies. Lumber was needed throughout the war to make props for the mines, telegraph poles, ship masts, railway sleepers, ladders, paper and even grave crosses for servicemen, and with the woodsmen away fighting, it was down to women to fill their boots.

LIFE IN CAMP

Around 4,000 WTC members were deployed around the British Isles, with many working in the south of England and throughout the isolated Scottish Highlands. Each volunteer spent two weeks at a training camp, where they were handed an axe and taught the essential skills for tree felling, snedding (removing the branches from felled trees) and loading logs onto tractors and trucks. They also learned to use a crosscut and bowman's saw, levers, cant hooks and other vital tools of the trade.

A lumberjill working for the Women's Timber Corps carries a log on her shoulder.

But nothing could prepare them for the spartan living conditions of the logging camps. Packed into communal – often freezing – wooden huts, running hot water was rare, with often the only heat coming from a cast-iron stove in the dining hall. Underpaid, and with most of their wages going on bed and board, it was the friendship and support of other members that helped many of the women to survive the mental and physical challenges of being a lumberjill.

FINAL SALUTE

Working from 7 am until 4:30 pm, and later in summer months, the lumberjills did dangerous and arduous work felling trees by hand, while teamsters worked with Clydesdale, Belgian and Highland Garron horses, which were used to drag the logs from the forest. Others sawed timber or drove the tractors and trucks. Working in all weathers, it was the WTC teams that helped to keep many of Britain's industries alive.

After the war ended, the WTC was disbanded in 1946, when each member handed back their uniform and received a letter from Queen Elizabeth, the Queen Mother. This acknowledgement aside, these committed members drew little praise or attention for their sacrifice and efforts, until a monument was finally erected in their memory in 2007. The dedicated memorial statue, *Salute*, stands in the Queen Elizabeth Forest Park near Aberfoyle in Scotland, in honour of every lumberjill who rose to the challenge, picked up an axe and helped to win the war.

INTO THE WOODS

The Women's Forestry Corps was set up in 1916 during World War I, and later became part of the Women's Land Army. By 1918, up to 3,000 women were working as foresters, producing timber for the war effort. The Women's Land Army was disbanded in 1919, reforming in 1939 for World War II.

Members of the WTC take a break from logging.

Two lumberjills use a crosscut saw to fell a tree.

LUMBERJILL TALES

Former WTC members share their memories at the unveiling of the Memorial Statue.

CHRIS FORRESTER

'We had no mechanical machinery to use; everything was done by hand. We chopped down trees with axes and crosscut saws, cut the timber into lengths, then loaded it onto tractors and trucks to be taken to the railway station.'

ELIZABETH MURRAY

'I signed up in 1942 when I was 17. I was at a camp in Buchan near Dumfries. There were four huts and we were lucky to have showers and running water. There was great comradeship among the girls. I don't think you get that same level of contact today using machines, but we used to really admire the trees we were felling. They were beauties.'

MARGARET GRANT

'We went out every day. For the first three months you just switch off: you're sore, hungry and tired. Then one glorious morning, you wake up to find you're a big, hulking brute and 66kg (146lb) of muscle

– and life is lovely! I worked a tractor, used the big saw in the mill, worked a horse, rafted timber. It was great fun. Not that I was ever weak, but it strengthened me a lot. It was lovely to work in the forest.'

MARGARET KERR

'There was lots of good company and fun to be had. We were well fed, but winter was bitterly cold. The cutlery was so icy we couldn't hold it, so we would dunk the handles in our tea. One night, one of the girls woke up to find snow inside her pillow.'

RITA ROBERTSON

'I was actually the replacement for a woman who was sadly killed by a tree that had fallen. I spent most of my time in the WTC on my knees, felling trees.'

TIBBY SCOTLAND

'I was a teenager when I was in the WTC, and life was good. Girls coming in from offices had never worked like that before, and it was wonderful being alongside them. It was hard work, and we weren't appreciated at all at the time, so it's nice to be recognised now. We weren't fighting soldiers, but we were bringing trees down.'

POETIC JUSTICE

Two poems featured in *Meet The Members: A Record Of The Women's Land Army*, 1945, capture the experience of the WWII lumberjills.

THE OTHER WAY

There is a land, or so I'm told,
Where timber girls ne'er feel the cold
Where trees come down all sned
and peeled
And there's no need an axe to wield
The transport's never broken down
And Jill's go every night to town
How different here in snow and sleet
Shivering with wet and frozen feet
But wait, the sun's come out at last
And summer's here and winter's past
The lumberjills work all the day
Who'd have it round that other way?

– Hilton Wood

FORESTERS

They're tramping through the forest
They're trudging through the mire
They're brushing past the undergrowth
They have but one desire
Their greatest thought, their highest aim
To see in Britain, Peace again
They have no tanks or rifles
They have no stripes or drill
They have no ships or aeroplanes
But Britain needs them still
They're fighting hard with axe and saw
They're Britain's 'Women's Timber Corps'
They're proud of their profession
Bad weather does not count
They bring the tall trees crashing down
The piles of pit props mount
They're doing their bit to win the war
This almost unknown 'Timber Corps'

– J I Melvin

THE WTC UNIFORM

On arrival to training, each new recruit would be allocated the following:

- 2 green jerseys
- 2 pairs of riding breeches
- 2 overall coats
- 2 pairs of dungarees
- 6 pairs of woollen knee socks
- 3 beige knitted shirts
- 1 pair boots
- 1 pair of brown shoes
- 1 pair of wellies or boots with leggings
- 1 green beret
- 1 melton overcoat
- 1 oilskin or Mackintosh
- 2 towels
- 1 green armlet and a metal badge
- 1 Bakelite hat badge

A statue commemorates the Women's Timber Corps Memorial in Aberfoyle, Scotland.

HOW TO

BE KING OF THE
⚒ LUMBERJILLS ⚒

Becoming a champion lumberjack or Jill isn't just about training and skill – you need to be mentally prepared, too. World champion lumberjill Martha King shares some of the secrets of her success

'When I picked up an axe at my first timbersports competition, people didn't expect too much from someone who looked like me,' says Martha King. 'For me to discover I had the timing and technique to best other competitors, including some of the guys, was so good. I felt like I'd found my place.'

People now know that they underestimate Martha at their peril. She's the current world champion lumberjill, women's US Stihl champion, world underhand champion, world singlebuck champion and world record holder in two underhand chop events. In other words, she's the fastest female woodchopper in the world.

Martha's first taste of competitive timbersports came while she was studying animal sciences at The Pennsylvania State University in 2007. Following in her father's footsteps, she joined the college team and was soon winning competitions. Showing an early flair for the underhand chop, her favourite event, she also excelled in sawing, axe throwing, pole climbing and chainsaw disciplines. 'I took to timbersports like a fish to water,' she says.

Martha's been around trees all her life and when she's not travelling the world and breaking records she works for her parents' tree service company in Chadds Ford, Pennsylvania, running chainsaws, pruning and felling trees, dragging brush and operating heavy equipment. She also spent five years working at a speciality hardwood lumber company sourcing and processing exotic woods for iconic luthiers (guitar makers) like Martin, Fender and Gibson.

'I grew up watching my father, Robert, apply a range of forestry practices in his professional career, and on our own property,' she says. 'I love my parents, and I wanted to do everything my dad did – but better!'

Martha competes in the axe-throwing event at the World Lumberjack Championships 2018 in Wisconsin, US.

While her family has always supported her dream to be a lumberjill, she's faced criticism from those who believe a woman's place isn't standing on a foot-thick block of pine. 'I've had women saying "girls should be girls" or telling me I should get a proper career, but I love what I do. I get to travel, meet incredible people and I have a great platform to inspire others.'

When old-school male competitors have expressed doubts about women woodchopping, Martha finds the most effective answer is a swing of her axe – not aimed at the naysayer in question (tempting), but smashing a block and busting another world record. 'If someone says women don't belong in timbersports, that's when my tenacity kicks in, and I go out and cut as hard as I can,' says Martha.

In 2019, that tenacity saw Martha chop and saw her way to the top of the tree in her best season yet. After winning the US Stihl Timbersports Championship, a week later she was crowned world champion

lumberjill at the Lumberjack World Championships in Wisconsin, one of the sport's most prestigious competitions, where she also became the underhand chop and singlebuck world champion. She now has the Sydney Royal Easter Show in her sights, and the Australian underhand title she's yet to win. 'I'm excited about what's ahead,' says Martha. 'I want to be a good example to people who think "I can't do that, because I'm too this, or not enough of that". I want to say if you're passionate about something, dedicate yourself to it, work hard, be the best you can be: there are no limits.'

Martha shares some of her motivational mantras:

FEED THE RIGHT BEAST

'There's a Cherokee legend that says we have two wolves fighting inside us – two inner voices – one is darkness and despair and the other is light and hope. The wolf that wins the fight will be the one you feed. Don't listen to your inner voice that is self-critical and beats you up – feed the right beast, the one that inspires you to keep going, stay positive and be better.'

DO THE BEST YOU CAN WITH WHAT YOU HAVE

'Remember, you're the only person who's equipped to be you. And you're responsible for living your life, so don't waste time comparing yourself to others. They are who they are, and you are who you are. Focus on becoming the best person you can be and embracing your best self. Be unashamedly you. Anxiety and feelings of inadequacy will try and creep in – don't let them.'

ABOVE: Martha's been around trees all her life as her family runs a tree service company.
OPPOSITE: Martha is the current singlebuck world champion.

HAVE AN ATTITUDE OF GRATITUDE

'I've worked hard, but I'm not here on my own merit. I've had so many people help me along the way. I can never thank my parents enough, or the university professors who believed in me. I also owe so much to timbersports pros Laurence O'Toole and Mike Eash, who've been so supportive with my training. They broke me down and built me back up better.'

MAKE TIME TO BE KIND

'No matter how long, or how hard, your day has been, don't take it out on others. Try a change of perspective. You never know what kind of day someone else might be having, and yours might be the only act of kindness they encounter. Even if it's just asking how the person at the checkout is doing, take time to engage in some meaningful conversation.'

YOU'RE NEVER TOO YOUNG TO TEACH

'Sometimes I help to train timbersports students and it might be their first time lifting an axe, but they'll often say or do something that'll make me think differently about how I do things. Everyone has something to contribute, so always keep your eyes, ears and mind open.'

DIARY OF A LUMBERJILL

Here's how woodchopping champion Martha spends her day.

6:30 AM

'I wish I could say that when I wake up in the morning, I crank out a workout, meditate and linger over breakfast, but I work my body hard, so between tree work and lumberjack training, I need all the sleep I can get! I push my snooze to the limit, do a few stretches, then get dressed, make breakfast and pack up my lunch. I don't like to eat too soon after waking up, so I take my breakfast along as well.'

7:00 AM

'I walk to work, as my parent's tree business isn't far. Each morning we're given the job scope for that day, anything from light pruning to removing trees with a crane. I'm usually paired with my little brother, Robbie, who is a very talented climber. It can be challenging and physically draining, but I love working with my hands on something tangible. It gives me an immediate sense of satisfaction.'

12:00 PM

'When it comes to nutrition, I rely on my body to tell me what it needs. Rather than stop for lunch, I tend to snack and hydrate throughout the day, enjoying first and second breakfasts – maybe an English muffin sandwich, fried chicken, salmon and rice, or a fruit smoothie. On an average work day, I walk 12.9km (8 miles), running saws and dragging brush. It's a great, full-body workout, so I can pretty much eat what I want!'

4:00 PM

'We usually finish work between 3:00–4:00 pm, but sometimes later in summer. Some days I rush to set up an underhand block in the fading light and chop (very carefully!) in the lights of my dad's log truck. When I have more time, I dedicate three hours to setting up, training, studying videos and adjusting my technique. My friend and mentor, Mike Eash, often trains with me, so it can become a bit of a social event, too.'

9:00 PM

'My training area is at my parent's property (where the wood stash is!), so I stop in at the house after my session. My mother, Katharine, often has a plate of food ready for me, and we share news from our day. After dinner, my dad will look over my shoulder at my training videos and tell me that he is faster and more precise, as I roll my eyes and laugh! Although by now it's late, I still have a garden to weed, vegetables to pick and a house to clean... but sometimes I scrap all that to take an evening hike under the stars.'

11:30 PM

'If I'm getting up early the next morning to travel to a competition, I'll make sure I have all my gear packed and loaded, Tetris-style, in the truck. And snacks! Lots of snacks! I take a shower, which feels like a luxury after a long day cutting trees, and to help my mind slow down, I'll read or listen to a podcast. I dedicate a lot of time to woodchopping, which is why I've been successful, but it's important to make time for other pursuits, which add to the fullness of life.'

CHOP! CHOP!

Martha's top tips for wielding an axe like a champ:

'The underhand chop was the first discipline I tried at university. Some people shy away from it as it looks dangerous, but when I picked up the axe for the first time, it felt so natural. There was a bit of trepidation, as I was swinging a heavy, super-sharp object between my feet, but once I got the hang of it, it was just love.

'Technique matters more than size: I'm 1.7m (5ft 8in) and weigh 59kg (130lb), so I'm tall but not a giant human. Chopping is all about how the axe meets the log, and balance and timing are key. If the axe is off-centre, and your body weight is unevenly distributed, the axe will not strike the log at the right angle. This will affect how the block opens up, and ultimately, the length of time it will take you to sever it. If you bring your hands together too soon at the top of your swing, the axe will be harder to control. Keep the axe in front of you as you begin your swing, keep your arms straight and pull it into the wood. The axe naturally wants to follow the arc into the block, but a tense mind and body will complicate this simple act. Believe me, working to get this right has been quite the pursuit! I use every bit of my body and height, putting my hands together and sinking into my swing at just the right time, bringing the axe head with explosive power into the block. People think it's just chopping, but it's actually quite an art form.'

Martha wins the 2019 Stihl Timbersports US Women's Division Championship.

LIGHTS! CAMERA! AXE-TION!

Loggers – and the tools of their trade – have starred in a rich mix of movies, from critically acclaimed film noir, to chronically bad schlock horror. Here are five to watch (not necessarily alone in a cabin in the woods)

THE ONE WITH THE CHAINSAW: *EVIL DEAD II*

Expensive, loud and heavy, a chainsaw isn't the obvious choice for a murder weapon. Yet since the late 1960s, it's been the torture tool of choice for many a filmmaker, roaring through flicks from Tobe Hooper's *The Texas Chainsaw Massacre* to Brian De Palma's *Scarface*. But without a doubt, the award for Unlikeliest Use of a Chainsaw goes to Sam Raimi's 1987 comedy horror, *Evil Dead II*.

After heading to an abandoned cabin in the woods for a romantic weekend with his girlfriend, Ash Williams (Bruce Campbell) unwittingly plays cantations from the *Necronomicon Ex-Mortis* (*The Book of the Dead*), unleashing a malevolent demon – and some notoriously slick camera work – as it whips through the forest.

A gore-fest of decapitation and chaos ensues, ramping up to a bloody crescendo which sees Ash chopping off his own possessed right hand, and strapping a customised chainsaw to the stump, before uttering the immortal line: 'Groovy!'

Meanwhile, the 'evil hand' is subdued beneath a bucket, weighed down with a copy of Ernest Hemingway's *A Farewell to Arms*, and a heavy dose of the black humour that made the movie a cult classic.

Ash wields his groovy chainsaw hand in *Evil Dead II*

'Here's Johnny!' *The Shining*'s iconic axe scene is one of the scariest movie moments of all time.

THE ONE WITH THE AXE: *THE SHINING*

A snowbound hotel, a sinister maze, a manically cycling five-year-old and an increasingly unhinged husband. No, this isn't a movie homage to home-schooling. Nor is it a scenario that screams: 'Happy vacay!' But as we discover by the end of director Stanley Kubrick's cinematic masterpiece *The Shining*, actress Shelley Duvall – who embraces the challenges that come with staying in Colorado's remote Overlook Hotel all winter – is nothing if not game. Her perseverance filming the infamous baseball bat scene 127 times before Kubrick was happy, setting a Guinness World Record for film takes in the

process, deserves at least a gold star.

Before the final credits roll on the 1980 adaptation of author Stephen King's novel, Duvall – playing Wendy, the wife of aspiring-writer-come-winter-caretaker of the Overlook, Jack Torrance (Jack Nicholson) – will find herself terrorised behind one of the most famous doors in film history (or, in fact, 60 of them: the number demolished before Kubrick approved the take). The iconic moment where a deranged Jack finally bursts through with an axe and greets his hysterical wife with a sinister 'Here's Johnny!' is considered one of the scariest of all time, while for Duvall, the entire filming experience was sheer… murder.

Howard Keel eyes up Jane Powell in woodchopping musical extravaganza, *Seven Brides for Seven Brothers*.

THE ONE WITH THE DUBIOUS WOODSMEN: *SEVEN BRIDES FOR SEVEN BROTHERS*

The eponymous brothers in this film kidnap some local lasses to be their wives and drag them back to their farm for the winter, expecting them to cook, clean and mend for them. If you can put aside your qualms about the premise – this is 1850s Oregon we're talking about – this bouncy musical about a family gang of lovelorn backwoodsmen is sure to lighten the mood.

Stanley Donen's 1954 classic stars Howard Keel as rough and ready woodsman Adam Pontipee and Jane Powell as Milly, whose log-chopping skills catch his eye while he's striding around town, singing *Bless Yore Beautiful Hide*, and looking to trade his beaver pelts for a bride: bingo!

Nominated for five Academy Awards, and winning the Oscar for Best Music Scoring of a Musical Picture, the film's expertly choreographed set pieces, including the lumberjack-tastic barn-raising scene and Lonesome Polecat – which sees the siblings singing about their singledom to the steady rhythm of their axes and saws – may just win you over, too.

THE ONE WITH THE WOOD CHIPPER: *FARGO*

If you ever need to dispose of a body with minimum noise and fuss, the method used in Joel and Ethan Coen's brilliant 1996 film noir *Fargo* may not be the one for you. Turns out that running a man through a woodchipper after killing him with an axe is mighty loud and messy work, especially when it's done in a snow-covered wood. Who knew? (Hopefully nobody reading this book).

In an Oscar-winning performance, actress Frances McDormand plays pregnant police chief Marge Gunderson, who discovers the gruesome scene while investigating a triple-homicide in Minnesota. In less bloody nods to the state's logging history, *Fargo* features a giant statue of Paul Bunyan with an axe looming above a highway sign saying: 'Welcome to Brainerd' – rumoured to be the home of the legendary lumberjack – while the movie's criminals stay at the Blue Ox Motel.

While the Bunyan statue is no longer there, film fans can catch him and Babe at Brainerd's Paul Bunyan Land, before recreating the woodchipper moment on a visit to the Fargo-Moorhead Visitors Center: Home to one of the most famous movie props in history, complete with a protruding leg.

THE ONE WITH THE DEMON LOGGER: *LUMBERJACK MAN*

Imagine Friday the 13th with a wagon of flapjacks and a pike pole, and you'll have a pretty good idea of what to expect from Josh Bear's 2015 comedy horror. All the standard slasher film tropes are here: a group of rowdy teenagers? Check. A summer camp in the woods? Check. An undead murderer with a lust for blood? Check. Plaid shirt? Check. Check.

But what's driving this demon logger to fell teens quicker than a Stihl MS 881? According to legend, it's wronged woodsman Nehemiah Easterday's insatiable desire to finish off his pancakes by Lent, slathered with the blood of his victims instead of syrup. Ahh, so now it makes total sense! 'This camp sits on the Sinkhole of Hell,' warns Dr Peter

Shirtcliff, the survivor of a previous syrup massacre, played by much-too-good-for-this-film actor Michael Madsen. Which makes you wonder which member of the committee had the bright idea of setting up a summer camp over a festering Hadean pit, when land surveys are so readily available.

But hey, who are we to question the illogical decisions made in a teen slasher movie? Without them, there would be no teen slasher movie. So on we romp, as the lumbering villain finds increasingly grizzly ways to chop down teens with his (quite expertly wielded) axe. With an appropriate soundtrack by Chainsaw, this is a fun one to watch with the lights out and a stack of pancakes. Just remember, in the words of the movie trailer: 'Don't get axed!'

Don't get axed! Lumberjack Man is on the hunt for pancakes.

CALL OF THE WILD

Lumberjacks weren't the only varmints roaming the forests of North America during the logging boom. Check out some of the animals they may have run into in the woods

MOOSE

Nothing can prepare you for its majestic beauty until you see one emerging from a stand of aspen or swimming across a rumbling river, its magnificent antlers cradling the skies above.

Like the lumberjack, these giants of North America encompass the spirit of wilderness and outdoor adventure. Found in the US and Canada, as well as parts of Europe and Asia, the moose is the largest of the deer species, growing up to 2.1m (7ft) at the shoulder and weighing up to 816kg (1,800lb), with antlers that can span 1.8m (6ft). Despite their size, they're fast runners, reaching speeds of 56 km/h (35mph), and excellent swimmers, known to submerge for a minute at a time.

While they're not naturally aggressive, moose will attack if they feel threatened, with bulls more feisty during the autumn mating season and cows becoming protective of their calves in late spring and summer, so always keep your distance.

MOOSE MUSHING
While moose haven't been widely domesticated, Albert Vaillancourt of Chelmsford, Ontario, trained two rescued moose calves to pull a sleigh, and toured Canada with his unconventional sled team in the 1940s.

GRIZZLY BEAR

An awe-inspiring predator, the grizzly is a North American subspecies of the brown bear, which is found in Asia and Europe. Mothers with cubs aside, grizzlies are mainly solitary animals and roam widely through forests, alpine meadows and prairies. While much of their diet consists of nuts, berries and roots, they also eat fish and animals, including rodents and even moose.

Measuring up to 1.5m (5ft) at the shoulder, the bears can tower up to 2.7m (9ft) tall when standing on their hind legs: a sight every lumberjack working in the backcountry hoped never to see. Luckily for the loggers, while most of their work was carried out the bears would be safely ensconced in their winter dens, but once the mothers emerged with their cubs in spring, the woodsmen had to be bear aware.

While the grizzly's size and power invoked fear, it also earned the animal great respect from the indigenous peoples – some tribes believe the bear is a deity and connected to the spirit world.

SPOT THE DIFFERENCE

Grizzlies and brown bears are generally larger than black bears, have a prominent hump at the shoulder, shorter ears, a concave or 'dished' facial profile and longer, straighter claws.

WOLF

The howl of a grey wolf in the night fills some with wonder and others with woe. This powerful apex predator has always invoked extreme reactions and split opinions.

America's forests and prairies belonged to the wolves before pioneers rolled their wagons into the West and the resulting demise of their prey species – bison, deer and elk – forced packs to target domestic animals for food. Hunted almost to extinction by the mid-1930s, wolves are now seeing a comeback in the US, with a successful reintroduction programme in Yellowstone National Park highlighting the vital role that they play in maintaining healthy ecosystems.

HOWL DO YOU DO?

Each wolf has its own unique howl, used to communicate with other members of the pack and to warn other packs away from their territory. The howl can carry up to 16km (10 miles) on open land.

Also found in Canada, Europe and Asia, grey wolves are highly social, living in packs of six to 10, led by an alpha male and female. The largest species of the dog family can stand up to 0.9m (3ft) tall and weigh up to 79kg (175lb). While they can survive for days without making a kill, they can also wolf down a whopping 9kg (20lb) of meat in one sitting.

BEAVER

Canoe any remote river in North America and if you're lucky, you'll hear the joyous slap of a beaver's tail. Nature's consummate lumberjacks are experts in plying their trade, gnawing through trees as deftly as a misery whip and building dams to rival any laid down by a river hog.

Found in North America, Europe and Asia, these semi-aquatic rodents are second only to South America's capybaras in size, weighing a stocky 27kg (60lb). Measuring up to 99cm (39in) in length, with a 30cm

BEAVERS BITE BACK

Eurasian beavers are being reintroduced to parts of the UK after they became extinct in the 16th century following hunting for their fur, meat and 'castoreum', a secretion used in food, perfumes and medicine.

(12in) tail, their streamlined bodies, webbed hind feet and rudder-like tail make them excellent swimmers, while thick fur protects them in icy waters. But most amazing, of course, are their teeth, which include four continuously growing, orange incisors.

Beavers live in family groups inside 'lodges,' built from branches and mud. Inhabiting a range of freshwater habitats, including rivers and ponds, they lead the way when it comes to landscaping. Not only will their dams slow down a river's flow, they'll also create wetland habitats, allowing other species to flourish.

WHITE-TAILED DEER

These fine-looking deer (also known as Virginia deer) are found across the Americas, parts of Europe and the Caribbean. Living in brushy, forested habitats, savannahs and agricultural landscapes, they grow to 107cm (42in) at the shoulder, and weigh up to 181kg (400lb).

In warmer months, they have a rich, red coat that turns greyish-brown in winter. They take their name from the white fur on the underside of their tail, which they flash when alarmed – warning predators that they've been seen – before darting for cover. They can escape at speeds of 48km/h (30mph) and clear 9.1m (30ft) in a single bound.

The bucks (male deer) grow impressive antlers in the summer and autumn and compete in sparring matches over territories and does (females), which give birth to one to three white-spotted fawns in spring. One of them you might know; he was the star of the Disney movie, *Bambi*.

HOW TO SURVIVE A BEAR ATTACK

You're out in the woods when a super-sized grizzly wanders your way. Do you: a) switch your phone to selfie mode; b) go in for a bear hug or c) wish you had paid more attention to that infamous six-minute scene in *The Revenant*? (Correct answer below)

While most forays into the wilderness will be happily incident-free, it makes sense to know what to do if you encounter a 318kg (700lb) grizzly. Most bears will run away at the terrifying sight of a hairy, plaid-wearing human, but if you catch one by surprise – especially a mother with cubs – it could feel threatened and attack. How you react could mean the difference between walking away unscathed or being left for dead like DiCaprio (thanks, buddies).

BE BEAR AWARE

The best way to survive a bear attack is to avoid it in the first place.

- *Never* enter bear country without bear spray – and know how to use it before you set off. Bear spray has a 6.1m (20ft) spread at a 7.6m (25ft) range and is the best deterrent for a bear attack; keep it handy in a holster.

- If you're in bear territory, be loud. Sing and clap your hands so that any bears know you're nearby and can leave the area.

- Avoid walking or working alone – when it comes to bears, there's safety in numbers.

- Don't zone out on your phone or wear headphones or earbuds – if there are bears around, stay alert.

- Be mindful of blind bends on your path and approach them noisily and with caution.

- Avoid venturing into dense bush and berry patches, where bears might be feeding.

- Never approach a lone cub or place yourself between a mother bear and her cubs. If she perceives you as a threat, she could attack.

- Never feed a bear and always make sure any food or toiletries are locked away safely in bear-resistant containers; they have a great sense of smell.

SURVIVAL MODE

You've done all you can to avoid a bear, but a big mama is eyeballing you. Keeping yourself – and the bear – calm is crucial.

- Never run: acting like prey will activate its chase reflex. Pick up any children immediately and group together.
- Quietly take up your bear spray and remove the safety lock. Remain still and calm, as you slowly position the spray.
- Speak to the bear in soothing, low tones to let it know you're a human.
- If it's stationary, move away slowly and sideways, so you can keep an eye on it and avoid tripping. Make yourself look bigger by moving to higher ground. If the bear follows, stop and stand still.
- Don't climb a tree – both grizzly and black bears are adept climbers – and don't drop your backpack: it could provide back protection should you need it.
- The bear may stand on its hind legs to get a better look – this means it's curious, but not necessarily threatening.
- Woofing, yawning, salivating, growling, snapping their jaws and laying their ears back are defensive bear behaviours.
- The bear may run towards you in a bluff charge, but only use the spray if it's within 6.1–9.1m (20–30ft) of you, or it won't work.
- If within range, follow the spray's instructions and use a sustained blast to create a cloud between you, adjusting for any wind. If the attack continues, spray directly into its face. Leave the area slowly after spraying.

NO BEAR SPRAY?

You've stayed calm and followed the rules, but a bear is about to attack and you've left the spray in the car. What do you do?

Grizzly bear: If you're attacked, play dead. Lie flat on your stomach and clasp your hands behind your neck. Spread your legs to make it harder for the bear to turn you over and remain as still as you can until the bear leaves you alone. Fighting back usually increases the attack's intensity, but if it persists, fight back using whatever you can to hit the bear in the face.

Black bear: In this case, don't play dead. Try to escape to a secure place like a building or car. If it isn't possible, fight back with anything you can, aiming at the bear's face and muzzle.

WALK. DON'T RUN
Adult grizzly bears can run up to 64km/h (40mph), so unless you're a greyhound, don't even think about outrunning a charging one.

Before entering bear country, always ask a local visitor centre or backcountry office for the latest bear safety information.

⚔ FEARSOME CRITTERS ⚔ OF THE LUMBERWOODS

We're not talking bears or bobcats. We're talking gumberoos, squonks and snoligosters. Be very afraid!

Maybe it's about living in a remote part of the world, or spending too much time in a forest. Perhaps it's a sign of an overactive imagination, or just a symptom of drinking too much moonshine. Whatever the reason, the world's wildest regions often give rise to myths of mysterious beasts – sometimes scary (Mothman, Wendigo), often hairy (Sasquatch, Bigfoot) and always with no hard evidence at all that they exist.

While lumberjacks came into contact with plenty of real-life beasts that could attack them (hello, Mr Grizzly), it was the tall tales told around the campfire that really put the wind up the woodsmen. The critters that filled the shanty boys' yarns made a bear encounter sound like a picnic. Loggers would move from camp to camp, sharing their stories of fantastic beasts of the forest. While some were clearly invented for scares, others manifested to make sense of the lumberjacks' world, adding humour and intrigue to the serious, sad or mundane. Here are a few to watch out for next time you go to the woods.

THE GUMBEROO

If you find yourself face-to-face with this hairless beast, remember that fire is your friend. While its thick, leathery skin renders it nearly indestructible, a flame will see it conveniently swell up and spontaneously – and loudly – explode.

THE SNOLIGOSTER

You'll find this crocodilian creature lurking in the swamps around Lake Okeechobee in Florida. It loves meat, tossing its victims onto the sharp spike on its back with a flick of its tail, where they'll stay until supper, when it grinds them up in a hole before inhaling or drinking them down.

THE HUGAG

Blessed with stamina to out-walk any hunters on its trail, this prehistoric moose-like beast can be found wandering America's lake states and Canada's Hudson Bay. It grazes on trees with its oversize lip and leans against them to sleep. Why? Its stiff, jointless legs render it unable to lie down.

THE HODAG

Hailing from Rhinelander, Wisconsin, this ugly critter has bulging eyes and a spiny back and has been known to sob loudly about its appearance. Luckily, a fear of citrus fruits means you can see it off with a lemon.

THE GUMBEROO

THE HODAG

THE SNOLIGOSTER

THE SQUONK

THE HUGAG

THE WHIRLING WHIMPUS

THE SQUONK

Home for this shy, morose monster is the hemlock forests of Pennsylvania, where it roams at dusk, eager to stay out of sight. Covered with lumpy warts and moles, it likes a good cry and is prone to dissolve in the flood of its own tears when looked upon, cornered or trapped.

THE WHIRLING WHIMPUS

Watch out when wandering Tennessee's trails. This gorilla-shaped being catches its prey by whirling around so speedily that it becomes invisible, while omitting a loud droning. On investigating, you'll be pulverised by its rotating paddle arms and licked up for its deliciously sticky supper.

HOW TO
BE A HIGH CLIMBER

Who better than world champion tree climber Stirling Hart to inspire you to climb to new heights?

Lumberjackin' wasn't all about chopping and sawing with your feet planted firmly on the ground. 'High climbers' or 'tree toppers' would use hooks and ropes to climb trees, with some species standing up to 91m (300ft) high, sawing off tree tops before the fallers went to work. After dinner, the toppers would challenge each other to see who could climb faster or higher – the inspiration for today's competitions.

Contemporary arborists and forestry workers still have a head for heights, chopping the tops off trees to reduce the risk of them falling in high winds, and spending up to eight hours off the ground, swinging from tree to tree in true Tarzan style. When he's not smashing world records or competing in timbersports championships across the globe, Canadian lumberjack and arborist Stirling Hart runs a forestry company, thinning trees for growth and fire protection around British Columbia.

A third-generation lumberjack – his family owned a sawmill, and both his grandfather and father were loggers and accomplished competitors – Stirling had his first rope, belt and spurs

(climbing spikes) aged four, and started scaling up to around 3m (10ft) trees. Fast-forward to 2010 and he claimed his first world record as a tree climber, racing up and down a 30m (100ft) tree in just 23.3 seconds.

In 2013, he broke the 27m (90ft) climbing world record with 18.3 seconds, and the 24m (80ft) world record with 17.81 seconds. Switching to chopping and sawing competitions in 2014, Stirling scooped further honours, before winning the Stihl Timbersports Champions Trophy in 2018, completing all four disciplines – stock saw, underhand chop, single buck and standing block chop – in under 65 seconds to win the title.

'Working in the forest is essentially what won me the competitions,' says Stirling, who was born near Vancouver and now lives in Squamish, where he also performs in a local lumberjack show. 'Climbing 83m (270ft) Douglas firs for a living is the best training and conditioning I could have. Being a lumberjack has allowed me to travel all over the world and meet amazing people. It's totally shaped my life.'

Stirling's top tree-climbing tips will take you straight to the top:

SET YOUR GOALS

'You need to have a goal in mind, because training is hard and you're going to find any excuse not to do it! Having a goal is the carrot you need to keep you motivated and focused – set yours as high as the trees you want to climb.'

LISTEN TO YOUR BODY

'A lot of people will run or weightlift as much as they can, but that doesn't always get the best results. In the run-up to a competition in July, I'll ramp up my training in February, go hard in April and May with gym work and sprinting, then wind down to give myself the chance to recover.'

ACCEPT THE PAIN

'Descending is far more dangerous than climbing up a tree, and at times I've hurt myself pretty badly. I've broken feet, twisted ankles, sprained knees, torn hip ligaments, displaced my pelvis, dislocated shoulders, lost skin on my forearms and knuckles, and had a *lot* of splinters. I also have a 13cm (5in) scar on my right cheek from when an axe fell out of a tree, narrowly missing my eye – it's become my trademark! But when you do well, it's worth it – the pain is part of the passion.'

BUILD ON EXPERIENCE

'When I was younger, I'd get nervous during a competition and think about screwing up. Now I know that as I put my

The world's fastest tree climbers can race up and down poles in seconds.

lot of weight on your knees when you're coming down the pole. My diet consisted of lean meat, whole foods, eggs and lots of vegetables. I'd drink lots of water, and supplement with protein, green powders and amino acids.'

STAY POSITIVE
'If you want to do well, you'll need to work on training your mind as well as your body. Losing is tough for everybody, but it's how you handle it that matters. Coming second in a competition actually inspired me to do better next time. Finding the motivation to stay on top is often the hardest part of winning.'

THE COMPETITION
Competitors race head-to-head up and down twin cedar poles of various heights, aiming for the fastest time. Starting with one foot on the ground and one beneath the orange marker line, on the starting signal they use climbing spurs and steel-core climbing ropes to scale the poles up to the height mark. They then quickly descend, touching the pole a specified number of times with their feet on the way down. In some countries, competitors belay back down the pole, rather than climbing.

---

all into training, I can only do my best. A little bit of adrenaline can help drive your performance, but try and find a way to keep your nerves in check. The more experience you have climbing, the more you'll increase in confidence and trust in your abilities.'

EAT FOR SPEED
'To be a great climber, you need to have explosive speed rather than weight, so clean food is what you need. When I was competing in tree climbing, I'd eat smaller meals, as it's not great to have a

ABOVE: Canadian Champion Stirling competes in the single buck discipline at The Stihl Timbersports Champions Trophy, 2018.
RIGHT: Stirling set the current springboard world record with a time of 35.67 seconds at the 2016 Stihl World Championships.

PRETTY IN INK

What better way to adorn those fine, woodchopping arms than with some striking body art? From retro Jacks and Jills to fierce forest beasts, the tattoo options for pledging your lumberjack allegiance are endless. Here's some inspiration if you're thinking about getting one of your own

ICE AGE LUMBERJACK

The oldest tattoos found on a person covered the frozen body of Ötzi the Iceman, who was discovered buried under glacier ice in Italy's South Tyrol in 1991. Scientifically dated to 3250 BCE, Ötzi had 61 tattoos in the form of lines and crosses, made by rubbing charcoal into fine cuts in his skin. The Copper Age mummy was found with a dagger, a bow – and an axe.

THE BIG SPRING DRIVE

The end of winter and melting snow signalled the start of the most dramatic – and dangerous – event of the year: the log drive

After a busy winter of chopping and sawing in the woods, the spring melt announced it was time for one of the most thrilling activities in the lumber calendar. Before logging roads and railways were constructed, millions of felled logs were floated down the rivers to the sawmills. Depending on the amount of timber and the river's length and layout, the journey could take days, weeks or months, with crews camping along the way, as they guided the logs to their destination.

Known as log drivers, river jacks or river pigs, the men who managed the drive were brave, hardy, agile and adept at keeping the timber moving through the raging rapids and around treacherous bends. Often riding the logs, with spiked – or caulked – boots to help secure their footing, they used peaveys to free up stuck logs and clear jams. Falling off could be fatal, with icy waters, hidden rocks and heavy trunks claiming many drivers who risked their lives working some of the world's mightiest rivers.

SKILLED CREW

With so much hanging on a safe and successful drive, good management was essential. Experienced members would go ahead to clear potential sticking points on the river, then the main body of the crew travelled with the logs, keeping them moving and quickly breaking up any jams. Younger, greener men followed towards the back in the 'rear crew', ensuring no logs were left behind, and freeing any strays with their pike poles.

On stretches of river lacking a strong current or lakes, the logs would be gathered together in a 'boom' – a floating log chain or barrier – and

HIGH & DRY

This phrase was first used to describe logs that became stuck on a drive where the flow of a river wasn't high enough to carry them all the way to the mill. This sometimes meant waiting until the following spring to get them moving again.

The last big log drive on the Little Fork River, Koochiching County, Minnesota, US, 1937.

winched along by a 'bateau', or small boat. Bateaux were also used to carry men out to reach stuck timber, but drivers would often leap on a log and simply ride it across the river to free up a jam, showing balance and skill.

A HERO'S WELCOME

The boss or foreman called the shots, employed for his knowledge of the river and ability to keep a crew of rowdy lumberjacks in check, both on the river and in camp each night. The spring drive would only start when he deemed the river ready, with a few sticks of strategically placed dynamite sometimes used to help break up thawing ice and set the logs on their way. A wooden raft, known as a wannigan, followed the drive, carrying tents, bedrolls and the drivers' gear, along with the cook, their helper, a stove and food provisions for the crew. After 10 hours of arduous river work, and

with the logs safely corralled for the night in booms on the river, the men sat down to a hearty meal in the dining tent, played music, told yarns and dried wet clothes around the fire. If they camped near a town or village, sometimes they'd show off their log rolling or 'birling' skills in an effort to impress the locals, too. And when the men and the logs finally made it to their final destination, there were celebrations all round. After braving the wildest of white water and risking all for the big drive, none were more deserving of a hero's welcome.

THE WORLD'S BIGGEST JAMS

Despite the skill and vigilance of the crew, log jams still occurred, with hotspots being the twists and turns of the river, sandbars, deadheads and rapids. Here are a few of the largest recorded pile-ups which drew crowds from miles around to witness the never-ending rivers of logs.

BELOW: The St Croix River OPPOSITE TOP: The Grand River. OPPOSITE: The Wisconsin River.

ST CROIX RIVER, MINNESOTA/WISCONSIN, 1886

Someone was likely sent to the naughty step for allowing this monumental jam to back up for a whopping five miles at the river's Dalles gorge, near Taylors Falls, on the Minnesota–Wisconsin border. An estimated 50 million board feet of white pine clogged the river for six weeks, with 400 men, two steamboats, horse teams and a 11kg (24lb) dynamite bomb finally managing to clear the 'jammedest jam,' as it was named by a local news reporter.

GRAND RIVER, MICHIGAN, 1883

When heavy rains overwhelmed the lumbering booms on West Michigan's Grand River, a huge jam threatened to decimate the state's logging industry. Canadian marine engineer John Walsh, who only had one arm, was heralded for breaking the congestion and averting disaster, preventing 37 million tonnes of logs floating into Lake Michigan and being lost. According to reports, the number of logs stacked up in 'The Great Log Jam of 1883' would have stretched almost 45,061km (28,000 miles) if laid end-to-end, enough to encircle the Earth once, with timber to spare.

WISCONSIN RIVER, 1884

Men worked for a month trying to clear this enormous log jam at Grandfather Falls, without success. The river drivers were moving around one million board feet of pine and while two-thirds made it over the falls in high water, around 32 million board feet were left high and dry. Eventually jam-breaker extraordinaire Jim Crane sent the logs on their way, working for two weeks with dynamite to free the wood.

DRIVERS ON FILM

For a glimpse into the life of a log driver, you can't beat the short film *La Drave (Log Drive)* by director Raymond Garceau. Produced by the National Film Board of Canada, the 1957 documentary features jaunty lumberjack shanties from Wade Hemsworth and follows the big spring drive along the river to a 'hungry timber mill' in Québec.

HOW TO
LOG ROLL LIKE A PRO

Follow these top tips from six-time world champion Shana Verstegen and you'll discover log rolling is easy as, er, falling off a log

ABOVE: 'River pigs' – the men who managed the drive – fight the foam of the Cleanwater River to move a white pine log, Idaho, US, 1961. OPPOSITE: A group of lumberjacks prepare for the log drive near Littlefork, Minnesota, US, 1937.

The sport of log rolling originated in the spring river drives of the late 1800s, when 'log drivers' or 'river pigs' guided and rode logs from the forest logging sites down the river to the lumber mill. Hard and perilous work, it brought regular soakings in icy cold water and the risk of being crushed in log jams, or even drowning.

The safe arrival of the logs and crew was always a cause for celebration, with locals coming out to meet the men to congratulate them on a drive well run. As the stars of the show, the lumberjacks would entertain their adoring audience with daring feats that displayed their logging skills, strength and bravery, competing in axe throwing, chopping competitions and, of course, log rolling. Two or three men would stand on a log and roll it out until just one was left standing, to be crowned the best 'birler', or log roller.

Honouring the log drivers' legacy today, men, women and children of all ages log roll in pools, ponds and lakes across the world, while pro-athletes compete in national and world championships, toppling opponents and records alike.

Born and raised in Madison, Wisconsin, Shana Verstegen has won six world championships – four for log rolling and two for boom running – and is a Great Outdoor Games and Stihl Timbersports Series gold medallist. She's also the co-owner of Madison Log Rolling, which runs programmes for kids and adults.

'Log rolling really is a sport anyone can do,' says Shana. 'You don't need to be particularly athletic, you just need to put some time into practice. And unlike some of the lumberjack sports, you don't need to be big or strong – in fact, some of the best log rollers are smaller, more agile competitors.'

Now it's your turn! Follow Shana's top tips and soon you'll be rolling like a champ.

1. 'The hardest thing when starting is finding the right kind of log and a body of water to roll it on. The logs we use are 3–4m (12–13ft) long and generally made from Canadian red cedar wood, although synthetic logs are becoming more widely available. While buoyant, they're also pretty heavy and hard to transport, so it's better – and safer – to learn at a club.'

2. 'When you first get on a log, make sure someone is holding it steady for you. Slowly stand up and find your centre of gravity. You may find it easier barefoot – once you have some experience, you can invest in spiked shoes, which help to increase traction on the log.'

3. 'Always look at the far end of the log. This will help you maintain your balance and condition you to look at your opponent's feet when you start to compete. If you take your eyes off the log, you'll fall in immediately – you've been warned!'

4. 'When you're ready to start rolling, move your feet up and down as fast as you can, as if the log's made of hot lava. Your brain can't react fast enough to the sudden direction changes of the log, so if your feet are already moving ahead of time, you'll be better prepared to react to the log's movements.'

5. 'Position your feet to find your balance and put your outside arm in front of your body to help stay centred. If you feel you're going to fall off, shift your body weight or change position.'

6. 'Now just keep marching. As you gain confidence, you can practise spinning, jerking, stopping and changing the log's direction to topple your opponent. But at the start, if you manage to stay on the log for more than five seconds, you're already a superstar!'

HOW TO SINK YOUR OPPONENT

'You need to gain control of the log at the right time to dislodge your competitor,' says Shana. 'Catch them off balance and they'll be susceptible to your attack. If their shoulders, hips or feet slip out of position, that's when to make your killer move. Remember, you're on the same log, so you're connected. To stop them attacking, you need to "lock up the log" by dipping your toes or your heels in the water – we call it boxing with your feet!'

OPPOSITE: World champion Shana teaches the art of log rolling in Madison, Wisconsin, US.

THE COMPETITION

Two log rollers stand on the same log, at different sides of a central dividing line that they cannot cross. Without any pushing or touching, they must try to knock the other into the water by rocking, spinning the log or splashing, unbalancing their opponent within a time limit. To win, they must dislodge their opponent from the log three times. The logs have varying diameters, with smaller ones rolling faster. But it's resilience and determination to get back up after each dipping that will really make you a champ.

THE LEGENDARY LUMBERJACK BIG JOE MUFFERAW

While the US has supersized Paul Bunyan, Canada has its own axe-wielding, river-driving hero in the form of rough 'n' ready woodsman Big Joe Mufferaw

The debate surrounding the existence of American lumberjack Paul Bunyan continues, but there's little doubt that Canada's own logging legend was based on a real-life bûcheron (woodsman). Joe Montferrand was born in 1802, in Montreal, Québec. Strong and agile, he became known as an outstanding athlete. He also often got into fights, dishing out hidings to local troublemakers and competing in boxing matches, knocking out the reigning Canadian champion aged just 16 in Québec City.

Standing 1.9m (6ft 4in) tall with blue eyes and fair hair, Montferrand loved the great outdoors. He joined the famed Hudson's Bay Company at 21, working as a voyageur, a dangerous job that involved transporting pelts along Canada's rivers by canoe, to satisfy the demands of the fur trade.

SHINER SHOWDOWN

In 1827, Montferrand began working as a lumberjack and river driver on the Rivière du Nord and the Ottawa River. Never one to shy away from conflict, he became a champion for the French-Canadian lumbermen who were caught up in violent clashes with Shiners – Irish immigrants who were eager to make their fortune from logging the Ottawa Valley's 'big timber'.

One tale recounts how he took on a crowd of 150 Shiners who ambushed him on the bridge between Hull and Bytown (now Ottawa). Undeterred by their number, he picked up the largest Irishman by his feet and swung him

A 4.9m-tall (16ft) statue of Big Joe stands outside the Mattawa Museum in Ontario, Canada.

JOS MONTFERRAND BÛCHERON LÉGENDAIRE
LEGENDARY LUMBERJACK

CANADA 42

around like a club, sending the leaders of the mob flying into the river, and the remainder fleeing the scene.

Later, Montferrand moved to Outaouais in western Québec, and after 1840 he worked as the foreman on log drives, until his retirement in 1857. After the death of his first wife, he married again in the spring of 1864, before passing away peacefully that October in Montreal. His son was born after his death, growing up to be as tall and strong as his father. Sir Wilfred Laurier, Canada's prime minster at the turn of the 20th century, described Montferrand as possessing 'undaunted bravery, muscular strength, thirst for danger and resistance to fatigue.' He also called him 'the most truly Canadian of all Canadians ever known'.

TALL TALES

A legend while he was alive, Montferrand's reputation continued to grow after his death, as writers attributed increasingly fantastical feats to his already impressive list of achievements. Published in 1884, his biography by Benjamin Sulte, *Histoire de Montferrand L'Athlète Canadien*, describes the woodsman as a 'homme extraordinaire', who personified a historic and honourable past. His popular folklore name came from mispronunciation, with non-French speakers interpreting his name as 'Muffero', 'Muffera' and the version that stuck, 'Mufferaw'.

He was included in two books by Joan Finnegan, *Giants of the Ottawa Valley* (1981) and *Look! The Land is Growing Giants* (1983), which reaffirmed his

reputation as a larger-than-life hero. Author Bernie Bedore further cemented Mufferaw's rightful place in Canadian culture in his popular book series *Tall Tales of Joe Mufferaw* (1979), *More Tall Tales of Joe Mufferaw* (1981) and *Mythical Mufferaw* (1994).

MAKING HIS MARK

Like Paul Bunyan, Big Joe is credited for influencing the landscapes where he logged, creating the Rideau Canal from the path he trod, while carrying his canoe to see his girlfriend; extinguishing a forest fire with five spitballs; and single-handedly constructing Mount St Pat. He also left his boot prints on 2m (8ft) high ceilings – one of his favourite tricks while impressing the ladies with his backflips. And just as Bunyan had Babe, Mufferaw's companion was a pet frog that was 'bigger than a horse and barked like a dog'.

In 1970, Big Joe made the leap from the printed page to the top of the charts, with a song by country music star Stompin' Tom Connors, which made it to number one. Entitled 'Big Joe Mufferaw', it mentions several tall tales about the lumberjack, including Lake Mississippi being formed from the giant's dripping sweat, and the time he fought 29 men in the Pembroke Pub after drinking a bucket of gin, 'leaving 29 boot marks ... signed with love.'

Like his fellow folk hero and strongman Bunyan, Big Joe Mufferaw has left his own indelible signature stamped on North America's landscapes, history and culture, too.

OPPOSITE: Joseph Montferrand was featured on a Canadian stamp in 1992.

POWER OF ART

The US Open Chainsaw Sculpture Championship brings together some of the world's best carvers, who spend four days transforming wood into works of art

'We like them sharp and running fast,' says Steven Higgins, talking about the tools of his trade: chainsaws. But Steven doesn't use his 50-strong collection to cut down trees – instead to carve intricate wooden artworks. Raised in Northport, Washington, in the shadow of the forests of the Pacific Northwest, Steven honed his skills during a seven-year apprenticeship with a master carver, which he began aged just 11 By 15, he started competing and has been travelling the world on the carving circuit ever since. Now based in Missouri, Steven's mesmerising *Mother Nature* sculpture scooped him the champion's title at the US Open event. 'It's all about finding the beauty of the wood and then figuring out how to let the natural tones play off each other,' says Steven. 'Wood carving is my natural habitat, and the chainsaw is almost an extension of my hand.'

The US Open Chainsaw Sculpture Championship takes place annually at the Wisconsin Logging Museum in Eau Claire.

In 2019, Steven won first place for *Mother Nature* (left). Corey Worden came in second for his sculpture of eagles (opposite, top, far left), while Chris Kuehn took third for his bear (opposite, middle, right). Fourth place went to Chris Wood for his wolf sculpture (opposite, bottom, far left).

HOW TO
LIVE THE

LUMBERJACK

LIFESTYLE

It's not just about wearing plaid and grooming your whiskers –
it's also about working hard, inner strength and a lusty appetite for
the great outdoors (OK, maybe it's a little bit about the cool shirts, too).
US champion Cassidy Scheer shares his tips for living
your lumberjack dreams

As the world's population becomes increasingly urbanised, spending more time indoors, stressed and sitting at desks, the appeal of spending time in the wilderness grows. For the men and women who work in the woods or compete in timbersports, being a lumberjack or Jill offers a lifestyle that not only encompasses the trademark look of the logger, but also offers a deep connection to the great outdoors.

Nobody is living this more authentically than Cassidy Scheer. The son of a four-times log-rolling champion, Cassidy held his first axe at age four, going on to star in family lumberjack shows, excel in log rolling and win 10 world titles in tree climbing. Switching to sawing and chopping, the Minnesotan won the Stihl Timbersports US Championships and

took silver in the Lumberjack World Championships just four years after qualifying for the US league.

'I love competing in these sports and enjoy the lifestyle that goes with it, which is about being healthy and active,' he says. 'Many people have climbed a tree, chopped firewood or maybe thrown an axe and, like rodeo, lumberjack sports draw on traditional jobs with an interesting history, which are aesthetically pleasing, too. I've lived in a city, so I understand the human need to reconnect with nature, and being a lumberjack offers so much pleasure: it's a great way of life.'

Lumberjacks relax in the bunkhouse at the Military Spruce Logging Camp in Hoquiam, Washington, US during World War I, 1917.

From learning the basics of holding an axe to competing in timbersports, Cassidy has embraced the lumberjack lifestyle since he was a child.

Want to make like a lumberjack or Jill yourself? Here are Cassidy's top tips for living the lumberjack dream:

GET OUTDOORS

'Growing up in a small, rural town in Wisconsin, surrounded by forests, lakes and rivers, I spent a lot of time outdoors hunting, fishing and skiing. I don't hunt now but still love being outside in nature, connecting with things that are more tangible and visceral. I spend a lot of time foraging for wild mushrooms. My favourite days are in spring and autumn, hiking through the state's magnificent white pine trees. I'll go out with a daypack and a cast-iron pan, catch a fish, forage some mushrooms and cook them up out in the woods. It's an amazing, immersive outdoor experience, and I love it.'

TRAIN SMART

'I'm constantly thinking about achieving the right balance in my training schedule, ensuring I do enough exercise to be as athletic as possible, but also refining my technique and how I present the axe and saw to the wood. The more you train in both areas, the better you'll be.

'Good mechanics on an axe swing or saw stroke will achieve more when you're cutting wood than just brute force, but once you've honed your technique, strength and power will help. I work on the movements used for chopping and sawing, such as explosive rotational power, which comes from the hips and core, and strengthening my legs. Cross-country skiing helps for endurance and hockey improves agility and hand-eye coordination. I do sprint training, weights and plyometric exercises to increase power and physicality, to be as fast, strong and agile as possible.'

STYLE IT OUT

'I really like an outdoor, refined style and traditional, rustic clothing brands like L.L.Bean, Best Made, Orvis and Filson. I've been into raw, denim jeans for a while and particularly love the flannel double-down look, layering different coloured

ABOVE, LEFT: The view from Cassidy's Scandi-inspired lakefront cabin.
ABOVE, RIGHT: Cassidy designed his lakefront cabin in Wisconsin himself.

and patterned flannels over each other. It's like matching two hardwoods on a piece of furniture. Wood always goes well with wood, no matter the colour or pattern. I went through a "metrosexual" phase at college, so I love the "lumbersexual" trend. I'm one of the louder, more flamboyant guys in the community. I do celebration dances and compete in red plaid tights, which has become my signature look, and also rock a mullet. If you feel good, you'll perform well, so my competition clothes need to be comfortable and allow for maximum mobility, too.'

EAT A BALANCED DIET

'I'm less meticulous about nutrition than other areas of my training because I'm a massive foodie and love rich, decadent and exotic meals! This usually takes precedence over eating the right amount of carbs and protein, although in the run-up to a competition, I pay more attention to the macronutrients consumed. I cut out junk food and eat cleaner, adding more fruit and vegetables, but still enjoy a glass of wine, a craft beer or brandy – it's all about balance. Wisconsin is the Dairy State, so I drink a lot of milk and eat around 4,000 calories a day, which I need to maintain my weight of 95kg (210lb). It was easier to party and recover quickly in my twenties, but I'm more results-oriented now, so I don't drink much before a competition – but we definitely celebrate when it's over!'

LIVE THE LIFE YOU LOVE

'My apartment is in the suburbs of Minneapolis, and I'm one of the few "urban lumberjacks". Here I can access nearby training areas and timber, and I'm near to another competitor, so we train together. But I love spending time at my lakefront cabin in Hayward, which I designed myself, taking inspiration from Scandinavian summer cottages. My main career is real estate, and I'm designing more cabins which will be for sale, but this is somewhere I escape to. Nothing beats a cabin in the woods as the perfect lumberjack hideaway.'

LUMBER CAMP CUISINE

With long days focused on logging, food was an important part of every lumberjack's life, providing fuel for forestry and a much-needed distraction from the backbreaking work

Labouring in the woods as a lumberjack for 10 or 12 hours a day was hungry work, with snow and rain adding to the demands on the body. The men needed plenty of food, or 'chuck', to power them through, and mealtimes were the highlight of the day, offering a break from the routine of chopping and sawing.

In the early years of forestry in Maine, where commercial logging in the United States began, conditions for the lumberjacks were brutal, with the remoteness of the camps hindering the supply of good, fresh food. Pork, beans and bread were the staple, cooked by a hired boy or sometimes by the men themselves. Other non-perishables in camp included baked codfish, pickled beef, flapjacks, sourdough biscuits, molasses and tea.

By 1870, 'all the common and substantial articles of food and drink' were on offer in the camps of the Great Lakes states, while in Canada a 'revolution in camp diet' took place around 1880. The food in the New England camps improved in the early 1900s after legislation was brought in. It's estimated most loggers consumed at least 5,000 to 6,000 calories a day, eating an early breakfast at camp, a morning snack and dinner (what we call lunch) out in the woods and a hearty evening supper (what we call dinner) at the camp when they returned.

BARRELS AND BELLIES

Feeding a large crew of loggers – with 75 to 100 men in camp – was a challenge. The cook and their assistant 'cookees' worked hard, toiling over an open fire or a cast-iron range, to keep serving pots and platters replenished.

BUNYAN'S KITCHEN

The myth of Paul Bunyan helped to carve out the image of the constantly hungry lumberjack. Raised on a daily diet of 50 eggs and 10 containers of potatoes, the logger's kitchen covered 10 square miles, while his insatiable appetite for flapjacks was legendary.

The dining room at a lumber camp near Effie, Minnesota, US, 1937.

The camp cook summons the men for their evening meal with his Gabriel horn in Effie, Minnesota, US, 1937.

Food was generally plain but wholesome, and the hungry lumberjacks devoured it all. Having a good cook in camp was a blessing, with poor chefs labelled as 'belly robbers' by the men. Mealtimes at camp were quiet, aside from the clanking of cutlery on metal dishes, with talking at times forbidden in the dining room or mess hall in an attempt to discourage fights. Time limits were often set for finishing food, too; the busy kitchen staff wanting the men away so they could move on to other tasks.

Historic records reveal the foods that shanty boys ate in camp. Between 1875 and 1878, the annual consumption of the 1,200 workers at California's Sierra Flume and Lumber Company included 75 tonnes of beef, 75 of flour, 10 of beans, 20 of potatoes, 5 of butter and 5 of dried fruit. In West Virginia in 1907, a smaller crew of 45 men ate a tub of lard, a sack of turnips, a sack of onions, a box of yeast, a case of cream, a barrel of sweet potatoes, seven sacks of Irish potatoes,

a case of pears, a case of peaches, a case of tomatoes, two cases of eggs, a barrel of apples, 51kg (112lb) of cabbage, a case of corn, 10kg (22lb) of cakes, 5kg (10lb) of tea, 12 cases of strawberries, two barrels of flour, 15 cans of baking powder and 136kg (300lb) of beef – in one week.

PINES AND PROVISIONS

An article titled 'Among the Michigan Pines', written in 1885 by Boston-native Charles Ellis for local newspaper *The Chicago Current*, noted that the lumberjacks he'd visited at a Michigan camp were healthy and ate well: 'The amount of work that a man or horse can do in the woods or elsewhere will depend entirely upon the amount of food that he can digest, over and above what is actually necessary to keep him in good condition in a state of inactivity. As regards these lumbermen, it is safe to say that they are physically strong and well, for only such can endure the work.'

In his column, Charles noted that the 55 men wolfed down the following provisions during 20 weeks in camp:

- 30 barrels flour
- 225kg (500lb) tea
- 22 barrels salt pork
- 1,814kg (4,000lb) fresh meat
- 15 barrels beef
- 68kg (150lb) baking powder
- 544kg (1,200lb) lard
- 181kg (400lb) butter
- 300 bushels potatoes
- 30 bushels beans
- 544kg (1,200lb) sugar
- 568 L (150 gallons) molasses
- 8 barrels crackers (hardtack)
- 6,000 pickles
- Cabbage, onions, turnips and other vegetables.

'This represents a great deal of eating,' noted Charles, 'but the work done will balance it off.'

WHAT'S COOKIN'?
Here is a typical day's sustenance in the lumber camp:

BREAKFAST
For breakfast, taken around 6:00 am, the camp cook would rustle up oatmeal or cornmeal with sugar or molasses, flapjacks (or pancakes), sausages, ham or salt pork, baked beans, biscuits, potatoes, doughnuts and prunes, all served with strong coffee.

NOSH NICKNAMES
Lumberjacks had nicknames for food, including gravel (salt), sand (sugar), stove lids or sweat pads (pancakes), cackleberries (eggs), doorknobs (biscuits), goldfish (canned salmon), logging berries (stewed prunes), Murphys (potatoes), redlead (ketchup), slush or blackjack (coffee) and swamp water (tea).

DINNER (LUNCH)
The loggers stopped for a morning snack of bread and molasses with tea and carried on working until dinner arrived at midday, sometimes served around a fire. Cookees delivered the meals in pails, riding a horse and wagon or a sled, known as a 'swingdingle'. This hearty meal was often a beef vegetable stew with potatoes, onions, carrots, turnips and cabbage, followed by pie and cookies. Ham and bean soup was also popular, served with more baked beans and sourdough bread.

SUPPER (DINNER)
When the Gabriel horn sounded to call the lumberjacks to dinner, the men would line up at the door of the cook shanty for a supper of meat (often roast or corned beef), potatoes, vegetables, bread or rolls, and desserts (usually pie or cake), along with tea or coffee. Then it was off to the campfire or men's camp to tell yarns, darn clothes, sing or play music.

A man eats a well-earned supper in Effie, Minnesota, US, 1937.

PAUL BUNYAN'S
FAMOUS PANCAKES

Make a breakfast fit for a legendary lumberjack with this hearty pancake recipe

According to lumberjack lore, Paul Bunyan's stove was the size of an acre, taller than a pine tree and it took a whopping 50 men to grease the griddle. What's more, the legendary logger could wolf down 50 of his favourite pancakes in one sitting. Elasticated pants at the ready? Let breakfast commence.

INGREDIENTS
Makes 12 small pancakes
- 120g (4oz) plain flour
- 80g (3oz) cornmeal
- 2 teaspoons baking powder
- 1 teaspoon baking soda
- 3 teaspoons sugar
- ¼ teaspoon salt
- 367g (13oz) plain yoghurt
- 2 large eggs
- 6 tsp butter, melted

HOW TO DO IT
1. Preheat the oven to 93°C (200°F). Whisk together the flour, cornmeal, baking powder, baking soda, sugar and salt in a large bowl.

2. In another bowl, mix together the yoghurt and eggs with a fork, then stir this into the flour mixture and add the melted butter.

3. Heat a large greased, or non-stick skillet until hot.

4. For each pancake, pour 4 tablespoons of batter into the skillet. Cook for three minutes until golden, then flip and cook on the other side.

5. Keep your pancakes warm by placing them on a baking tray or cooling rack in the oven while you cook the rest.

6. Serve with warm syrup, or add fruit and other toppings of your choice.

LAUREL FORK SAPSUCKERS
APPLE BUTTER

You can almost taste the autumn leaves in this rich apple butter, made from an old family recipe at the Laurel Fork Sapsuckers Sugar Camp, high in the Appalachian Mountains of western Virginia

Surrounded by native red spruce forest, the Laurel Fork Sapsuckers Sugar Camp is known for its delicious pure Virginia maple syrup, made using traditional tree-tapping methods and wood-fired flat pans. The sustainable tree farm also produces a mean apple butter, perfect for spreading on toast or smothering over pancakes. Here's how to make it.

INGREDIENTS
Makes around 1.7 litres (60 fl oz)
- 15 cooking apples
- 3 tablespoons granulated sugar
- 3 tablespoons brown sugar
- 2 teaspoons cinnamon
- A pinch of ground cloves
- Splash of bourbon or lemon juice

HOW TO DO IT
1. Peel and slice the apples, then chop the slices into smaller pieces, known as 'snits'.

2. Add the snits to a pan with a splash of water and cook until the juices have come out, stirring continuously so the mixture doesn't burn.

3. Add the sugar and spices, and simmer on a low heat until the apple butter is thick enough to hold its shape on a spoon and deep caramel in colour. This should take around an hour.

4. Add a splash of bourbon or lemon juice to zing up your sauce.

5. Pour the apple butter into glass airtight jars and keep in the fridge for up to two weeks.

6. Spread the apple butter on toast, stir a dollop into your cereal, eat it with cheese or use it as a topping for pancakes or waffles.

SPRUCE UP YOUR LIFE

If you ever find yourself lost in the woods, never fear.
A simple spruce brew will not only help you stay warm,
it will give your immune system a boost, too

Ever wondered how you'd survive alone, without food or a phone in the forest? Spruces and pines have long been used by indigenous peoples as a food source, for making drinks and for healing (trees with ancient bark-peeling scars are still common in old-growth pine forests), so these prickly powerhouses could save the day if you find yourself in a tight spot. Many parts of the trees are edible, from the inner bark – which is packed with stored carbohydrates, dietary fibre and minerals – to the pollen and pine cone seeds, and the needles are a great source of vitamin C.

POWERFUL POTIONS

Canada's First Nations people were making spruce drinks for generations before French explorer, Jacques Cartier, arrived on his second voyage to the New World in 1535. When scurvy broke out, killing 25 of the 110-strong crew, Domagaya, the son of Iroquois chief Donnacona, showed the sailors how to make a vitamin C–packed potion from local pines. Believed to be spruce beer, the brew saved the lives of the remaining men. Cartier repaid them in true colonial style, kidnapping Donnacona and nine of his tribe, including his sons, and sending them back to France, where all but one died.

VITAMIN TEA

Steep a spoonful of chopped pine or spruce needles in a cup of hot water for 10 minutes to make a tea that's packed with vitamin C. Just one cup contains as much as five times your daily requirement.

A group of First Nations men in Ontario, Canada.

BIG-TIME BREWERS

- British explorer Captain James Cook made spruce beer in New Zealand during his second voyage in 1773, boiling spruce branches and tea plants with yeast and molasses.
- The first President of the United States, General George Washington, served spruce beer to his troops in 1775 at the start of the American War of Independence.
- United States founding father Benjamin Franklin made up a brew from essence of spruce and lots of molasses, which inspired modern craft beers.

HOP TO IT

In her 1796 book *American Cookery*, which features Native American recipes, Amelia Simmons describes how to brew a spruce beer:

- Take four ounces of hops, let them boil half an hour in one gallon of water, strain the hop water, then add 16 gallons of warm water, two gallons of molasses, eight ounces of essence of spruce, dissolved in one quart of water.
- Put it in a clean cask, then shake it well together, add half a pint of emptins [yeast or leavening], then let it stand and work one week. If it's very warm weather, less time will do. When it is drawn off to bottle, add one spoonful of molasses to every bottle.

VIKING VA-VA-VOOM

Ancient Scandinavians brewed beer from the young shoots of Norway spruce trees, convinced it increased their fertility and strength in battle.

NATURAL REMEDY

Spruce needles have traditionally been used as an antiseptic, expectorant, antibiotic and sedative.

CANOE GLUE

Indigenous people used the sap from the spruce trees as glue for their birch bark canoes, while lumberjacks would chew on it like gum to freshen their breath.

BESTO FOR PESTO

The young spruce tips that grow in spring can be used raw in salads or pesto, or cooked to make syrups and jams and flavour dishes – they're especially good in Thai cuisine.

WARNING: PICK YOUR PINE

Before you go a-foraging in the woods, make sure you know your pines. Not all species are safe to eat – including the Norfolk Island pine, the yew and ponderosa pine – so correct identification from a reputable tree book or guide is crucial. Always consult a medical professional before using any kind of plant for healing, and pregnant women should avoid eating or drinking pine or spruce needles.

HOW TO
EAT LIKE A CHAMP

Want to build some lumberjack-sized strength and agility?
It's not all about stacking steak and eggs for breakfast.
Fitness expert, author and founder of Fit Men Cook
Kevin Curry shares his healthy tips for eating like a champion

build and recover muscle tissue. But lumberjacks aren't bodybuilders (even though some may look the part), so you want to have a balanced amount of fat in your diet, too.'

BUILD MUSCLE, STAY AGILE

'Swinging an axe consistently for an hour will burn around 350–500 calories, and the average male lumberjack eats around 4,000 a day to get in competition shape, while competing females will eat around 2,500–3,000 a day. For both, I'd recommend starting with 2.5g of protein per kilogram of body weight, 4–7g of carbs and 0.5–2g of fat for that kind of work. That's similar to how bodybuilders eat to put on massive muscle, while staying lean enough to be agile.'

RETHINK THE 'LUMBERJACK BREAKFAST'

'Let's reconsider the lumberjack's breakfast. Here in America, some diners have created "lumberjack-themed" breakfasts that are high in carbs and fat and low in protein. Essentially, the protein and fat distribution needs to flip. Instead, try something like my High-Protein Egg, Yam and Cheese Jar. It's effortless to make (and eat on the go!), and also has a much healthier split, with 41g of protein, 45g of carbs and 15g of fat.

P hiladelphia-born fitness expert Kevin Curry overcame severe depression and weight issues by turning to healthy eating and a diet packed with tasty nutritious foods. Along with a popular Instagram account and YouTube channels, Kevin has a FitMenCook app, which has reached number one in the health category in over 80 countries, and a best-selling book, *Fit Men Cook*. So he knows his stuff about about proteins, micronutrients and all the good stuff lumberjacks should be loading in between.

STRIKE A BALANCE

'Whether you're training at an Olympic level or just starting to think about your nutrition more seriously, it's essential to understand the different kinds of calories out there. Wielding saws and axes means you're going to require a high-carb diet to fuel you throughout the day, with a healthy complement of protein to help

OPPOSITE: Men at a logging camp near Effie, Minnesota, US dish out and serve food, 1937. TOP: Kevin designs recipes that help to build healthy bodies. RIGHT: Plant-based meals pack a protein punch that's just as effective as red meat, poultry or fish.

Salisbury mushrooms and peas is a dish that follows the guidelines of the Mediterranean diet.

CHALLENGE STEREOTYPES

'Lumberjacks have an image in our culture: they're big, burly, bearded and they eat a dozen eggs and a pack of bacon for breakfast. But stereotypes often don't do anyone any favours. Alternative sources of protein can work just as effectively as red meat, poultry or fish. Not only are plant-based sources, like peas, edamame and beans, more sustainable, but you can also use them to make delicious meals that pack a protein punch, while helping you maintain a balanced diet. I enjoy bodybuilding and high-intensity interval training, and my muscles definitely didn't shrink on my four-day High-Protein Vegan Meal Plan, so I promise yours won't either!'

EMBRACE THE MEDITERRANEAN

'I started by focusing on macronutrients, because that's where we begin when we're discussing dieting or setting nutrition goals for specific purposes. But micronutrients are just as essential, which is why it's time to say goodbye to a "meat 'n' potatoes" lifestyle. Here's why I love the Mediterranean diet so

much, and why it's still the reigning diet year after year. Not only is it easy to maintain as a lifestyle, but it's also full of bright, vibrant and flavourful foods, like cucumbers, tomatoes and red onions, that help to ensure your body's getting all the vitamins and minerals it needs. Plus, it never gets boring. And if there's one thing I can't stand, it's eating boring food!'

HIIT THE TOP

'Now let's get outside of the kitchen for a minute and think about using our bodies to stay healthy, build muscle and get into great competitive shape. High-intensity interval training (HIIT) workouts are fantastic ways to build muscle, because the movements involved usually activate a wide variety of muscles all at once – not unlike competitive lumberjack sports, or the daily demands of the logging profession itself. You won't gain the same kind of muscle mass you'd build benching your one-rep max, but you will tap into highly effective, even explosive power.'

ADD A KICK TO YOUR H2O

'Lastly – and this is probably the most important tip – remember to stay hydrated. Drinking enough water throughout the day prevents injury by protecting your joints, keeping them lubricated and dispersing nutrients throughout your body. Hydration is so overlooked, but so important that I even include a water-tracking feature in my app. If you're struggling to stay committed to drinking water throughout the day, try adding some mint leaves, which will give it a refreshing kick (and freshen your breath, too), or even more creative ingredients like jalapeños: spicy, but as a lumberjack or Jill, you can take it!'

THE HEALTHY
LUMBERJACK BREAKFAST
HIGH-PROTEIN
EGG, YAM AND
CHEESE JAR

INGREDIENTS
Makes 1 serving
- 100g (4oz) yam (or sweet potato)
- 2 eggs
- 3 egg whites
- Pinch of sea salt
- 1½ teaspoon herb seasoning
- 32g (1oz) diced red pepper
- 2 tsp diced red onion
- 43g (2oz) shredded spinach
- 32g (1oz) reduced-fat shredded parmesan cheese (optional)

HOW TO DO IT
1. Peel then grate the yam into a bowl and set it aside.

2. In a separate bowl, beat the eggs and egg whites with the salt and herb seasoning.

3. Add the pepper, red onion, spinach and a little parmesan (if desired) to the eggs, and mix together.

4. Spray an ovenproof jar (at least 355ml [12oz] in size) with olive oil, then add the grated yam. Pat it down so it covers the bottom of the jar.

5. Pour the egg and veggie mixture into the jar, then garnish with a sprinkle of parmesan.

6. Place the jar on a baking tray and bake in the oven for around 30 minutes at 190°C (375°F).

HEALTHY FORESTS, HEALTHY PLANET

The 19th-century logging boom changed landscapes across North America, and deforestation remains an issue of global concern today. Can sustainable forestry balance the economic benefits of timber with the environmental value of trees?

Since the first English settlers arrived in Jamestown, Virginia, in 1607, it's estimated that America has lost somewhere between 75 and 90 per cent of its virgin forest. Indigenous peoples farmed holistically and were hunter-gatherers, working in harmony with the land, but the new arrivals voraciously tore through the New World, converting ancient forests to farmlands, and logging like there was no tomorrow. In some regions, all that remained were vast areas of 'cutover', a barren landscape of stumps, stripped of all life.

Legal forest and land protections, introduced in the mid-1800s and subsequent years, arrested what could have been total annihilation. The world's first national park, Yellowstone, was established in 1872, and the preservation of its two million acres is the reason the UNESCO World Heritage Site remains one of the few intact ecosystems on Earth today. Elsewhere, a fragile balance remains in play.

ANCIENT FORESTS

United Nations data shows there are more forested lands in North America today than 100 years ago, and between 2010 and 2020, forest cover in the United States increased 0.03 per cent annually. Meanwhile, according to the Canadian Forest Service, the area harvested in 2018 represented 0.2 per cent of the total area of forest land, with the harvested area promptly replanted.

Leaving carbon 'locked' in the forest is a good idea. The Pacific Northwest is home to some of the highest carbon density forests in the world, where trees can store carbon for more than 800 years. Stretching from northern California to Alaska, this is where you'll find some of America's last

FORESTS TO FARMLAND

While unsustainable and illegal logging are having a devastating effect on the world's forests, the biggest global driver of deforestation is agriculture: converting forests to farmland and grazing land for livestock.

ABOVE: A forest in British Columbia, Canada where harvested areas are quickly replanted.
BELOW: A truck hauls salvaged logs from Montana's Lolo National Forest, US. Salvage logging recovers trees damaged by storms or fires.

remaining old-growth forests, which are still actively targeted for logging.

A 2018 report by researchers at Oregon State University and the University of Idaho found that logging is by far the number one source of greenhouse gas emissions in Oregon, emitting 33 million tonnes of CO_2 a year, almost as much as one of the world's dirtiest coal plants, the Taichung Power Plant in Taiwan.

In 2019, the Centre for Sustainable Economy concluded that the logging industry emitted enormous quantities of the greenhouse gas. Focusing on the industry in North Carolina, the study found that 201,000 acres of forest are cleared each year, producing 44 million tons of carbon dioxide. The United Nations Food and Agriculture Organization (FAO), meanwhile, estimates that the world has lost around 420 million hectares of forest since 1990, mainly in Africa and South America. And while trees are being replanted, industrial forest lands store much less carbon than the native forests they've replaced, and sustain less biodiversity – one million species are known to be at risk of extinction. The good news is that now the data is out there, the damage can begin to be repaired. The ancient forests that have been lost will never return, but with hindsight and new science on our side, we can plant the seeds of a greener tomorrow.

Conservationist John Muir protected America's wilderness.

SO WHAT IS SUSTAINABLE FORESTRY?

According to North America's Sustainable Forestry Initiative (SFI), which works with the forest sector, conservationists, governments and communities to advance the sustainable use of forest lands, sustainable forestry ensures the long-term health of forests while providing social, economic and environmental benefits from timber harvesting. Management decisions and activities are based on scientific research, rigorous planning processes, certification standards and meaningful public consultation. They also support ecosystem services, like water purification and carbon storage, while maintaining the health and diversity of forests. Replanting after harvesting trees helps forests, and the habitats they contain, to regenerate. This is one of the core principles of sustainable forest management.

MAN OF THE WILDERNESS

Known as the 'Father of the National Parks', Scottish-American author, botanist and early conservationist John Muir helped to secure protection for America's wilderness areas, including Sequoia, General Grant and Yosemite National Parks and Yosemite's Mariposa Grove, a magical forest of 500 giant sequoias, home to the 3,000-year-old 'Grizzly Giant'.

In his essay, *God's First Temples; How Shall We Preserve Our Forests?*, published in 1876, Muir warned of the dangers of destroying forests, 'the most destructible of the natural resources'. In a brilliant early analysis of trees' contribution to the Earth's 'climate, soil and streams,' he warned: 'Our forest belts are being burned and cut down and wasted like a field of unprotected grain, and once destroyed, can never be wholly restored.'

Going on to found the Sierra Club in 1892, to 'do something for wildness and make the mountains glad,' Muir helped to preserve precious habitat and inspire awe and admiration for land that the country's Native people had been protecting as responsible stewards for thousands of years.

Loggers are key players in helping to solve some of today's biggest sustainability challenges.

WHY DO WE NEED FORESTS?

Forests are one of the planet's most important natural resources. They're the ultimate 'renewable' and one of the greatest tools in fighting climate change. They clean the air we breathe, filter the water we drink and support educational opportunities for today's youth.

HOW DO TREES FIGHT CLIMATE CHANGE?

Protecting the world's trees is one of the most cost-effective forms of climate action. Forests act as carbon sinks, absorbing roughly two billion tons of carbon dioxide each year. They're also increasingly managed for resilience in the face of climate change's effects. Practising climate-smart forestry focuses on actions like increasing the diversity of tree species to make them more resilient to wildfires and pests. According to the US Forest Service, 100 trees remove 48 metric tonnes (53 tonnes) of carbon dioxide and 195kg (430lb) of other air pollutants every year. If we want to tackle the issues of climate change, water quality, waste reduction and species loss, taking good care of the world's forests is fundamental.

HOW DOES THIS 'GREEN' APPROACH HELP COMMUNITIES AND WILDLIFE?

Sustainable forestry is focused on encouraging a positive relationship between people and forests, balancing their needs, and aiming to create both a sustainable marketplace and healthy landscapes. Purchasing products from a sustainably managed and certified source helps to conserve the planet's precious wildlife and natural resources.

Communities rely on forests for their livelihoods and economic development, sustainable products, recreational benefits and human health. These links have always been important, but are even more relevant in today's increasingly connected and developing world.

HOW DO LOGGERS PRACTISE SUSTAINABLE FORESTRY TODAY?

Logging companies need to ensure they're implementing forestry practices that protect the environment every day. Sustainable management enhances water quality, protects wildlife habitat, accounts for wildfire risk, counters invasive species and recognises indigenous rights, accounting for the social and economic wellbeing of workers and local communities.

Forest certification standards, such as the international Forest Stewardship Council (FSC) and the SFI, are there to help ensure forests are managed sustainably. The SFI trains thousands of loggers in sustainable forest practices each year. When they're aware of the importance of their role and responsibilities, they're better equipped to protect the environment.

THE JUMPING FRENCHMEN OF MAINE

When a mysterious affliction spread through a remote logging community in New England in the late 1800s, Dr George Millard Beard ventured into the woods to investigate ...

George M. Beard.

'They could not help striking their best friend, if near them, when ordered... It was dangerous to startle them in any way when they had an axe or knife in their hands ...'

While it could easily be the screen direction in a script for the latest lost-in-the-woods-teen-slasher, this alarming description is actually from an American neurologist, based on his own observations of a strange phenomenon he experienced in an isolated lumberjack camp in Maine.

Rumours were emerging from the forests of New England, about a community of French-Canadian loggers suffering from an unexplained syndrome, which caused them to exhibit an extreme reaction when startled. At the annual Meeting of the American Neurological Association in 1878, Dr George M Beard announced his intention to visit the logging camp in Moosehead Lake to observe and examine the afflicted.

LIFE ON A KNIFE EDGE

Known as 'The Jumping Frenchmen of Maine', the lumberjacks demonstrating the syndrome displayed an exaggerated response to loud noises, sudden commands or unexpected contact. The reactions ranged from screaming, to flailing their limbs, hitting things or people, throwing objects and, of course, jumping. They would also often repeat an order they'd been given like a parrot (a condition called echolalia), while making violent, muscular movements. Reporting on his findings at the camp, Dr Beard observed: 'Whatever order was given to them was at once obeyed. Thus one of the Jumpers who ... was told to throw [a knife] ... threw it quickly so that it stuck in the house opposite [and] at the same time, he repeated the order to throw it with a cry of alarm ... He also threw away his pipe, which he was filling ... when he was clapped upon the shoulder.'

JUMPING TO A CONCLUSION

Of the 50 people Dr Beard observed, he found 14 cases of the syndrome in people from four families, suggesting a possible genetic link, although this wasn't proven. Certain medical conditions can cause excessive startling, such as magnesium deficiency, tetanus or degenerative brain disorders, but Dr Beard speculated that the syndrome had developed due to the impact of living in remote isolation in camp. He also suggested it started in childhood, lasted a lifetime and was more prevalent in men. The condition itself didn't harm the Jumpers, but such extreme reactions could sometimes put them – and those around them – in danger.

'Two Jumpers standing near each other were told to strike, and they struck each other very forcibly,' Dr Beard recorded. 'When the commands are uttered in a quick, loud voice, the Jumper repeats the order ... They could not help repeating the word or sound that came from the person that ordered them, any more than they could help striking, dropping, throwing, jumping or starting.' The men didn't just respond to commands or human voices. Any loud or sudden noise could spark a reaction. As Dr Beard noted: 'It was not necessary that the sound should come from a human being ... One of these Jumpers came very near to cutting his throat while shaving on hearing a door slam. They have been known to strike their fists against a red-hot stove, to jump into fire and into water.'

EXTREME SURPRISE

While humans have an inherent 'startle response', there are several conditions that manifest a more extreme reaction to outside stimuli: hyperekplexia, a rare neurological disorder that causes patients to go rigid when surprised, sometimes falling face first onto the floor; startle epilepsy, when those affected experience seizures triggered by a sensory change such as taste, sound, pressure or temperature; and the rare 'jumping' reaction, experienced by the lumberjacks in Maine and a few other communities across the globe. The condition was reported in other remote lumber camps in

STEAM POWER
Moosehead Lake is the largest lake in Maine. In the early 19th century, it was the only way to reach many of the state's remote logging camps, with early steamboats hauling supplies and passengers to the camps, and towing booms of logs to the sawmills.

New England and Québec at that time, while similar variations include 'latah' in Malaysia, 'miryachit' in Siberia and Louisiana's 'Ragin' Cajuns'.

CULTURAL CONDITIONING

Studying Dr Beard's findings, French neurologist Gilles de la Tourette came to believe that the syndrome was part of the same group of illnesses as Tourette's, which affects the nervous system and is characterised by compulsive motor and vocal tics. While some of the jumping behaviours are similar to those exhibited by people with Tourette's, extreme stress, emotional tension, fatigue and even cultural conditioning could also be factors to consider.

As recently as 2011, 19 students and one adult at a school in Le Roy, New York, started exhibiting mysterious involuntary twitches, tics and spasms. While just one student was diagnosed with Tourette's Syndrome, the others who had been displaying similar behaviours were diagnosed with conversion disorder.

Doctors concluded that psychological stress had caused the patients to suffer physical symptoms and mass psychogenic illness: the group, it was suggested, had been subconsciously copying each other. A rest from stress and social media was prescribed, along with treatment at a neurology clinic, and life returned to normal.

While building an Instagram following may not have been a concern for the Jumping Frenchmen of Maine, the hardships that they experienced working in one of North America's most remote

regions may have been enough to trigger the strange syndrome, which scientists are still striving to understand today.

JUMPERS UNDER FIRE

Robert E Pike, who wrote about life in the lumber camps of New England in his 1967 book *Tall Trees, Tough Men*, told how the Jumping

Frenchmen of Maine often found themselves the victims of practical jokes at the hands of the other lumberjacks.

'If a Jumper was shaving, or whistling, or just sitting on a riverbank, and someone came up behind him suddenly and cried: "Jump into the river!" (or "into the fire", if there was a fire), in he'd jump.'

If the camp cook was a Jumper, 'the men would wait until [the cook] was about to place a dish of soup or some other spilly food on the table and then say, "Drop it!" and down it would come, right down the neck of the nearest man.'

Sometimes a lumberjack would pretend to strike the man sitting next to him. 'Every Jumper in the line would turn and strike at his neighbour. Or a man would pretend to throw his pipe on the floor. Then the Jumpers could not help dashing down their own pipes.'

A team of lumberjacks posing with a felled giant redwood tree, California, US, 1905.

PILE HIGH CLUB

Gary Tallman may have the most artistic farm in Montana, thanks to the amazing mosaics he creates with the logs in his woodpile

Nestled amid the pines and aspen of the Little Belt Mountains in Montana, Gary Tallman's farm holds a lumber-size secret: a 2 x 4m (8 x 13ft) mosaic, constructed from wood gathered in the local forest. These ornate log piles have made Gary somewhat of a local celebrity, although the modest octogenarian fails to see what the fuss is about.

'I started building them just because I enjoyed doing it, and to send photographs of them to my grandkids,' he says. 'It surprises me that people are fascinated by them. I never expected it to go this far. It's kind of embarrassing sometimes.'

Preferring to keep his unique creations personal, Gary has twice politely declined invitations from the local Paris Gibson Square Museum of Art to create exhibition works.

With changing themes and motifs each year, the mosaics take Gary around 20 hours to make – not including the hours spent gathering, chopping and sorting the wood, or drawing his preliminary sketches. Featuring owls, bears, mountains and trees, Gary's art is inspired by the surrounding wilderness and wildlife, and uses different-coloured wood species, including cedar, larch, poplar and cottonwood, to create the designs.

'We've always admired our woodpile, and there are so many tones in the timber,' says Gary's wife, Marilyn. 'Gary sees beauty in all kinds of things.' It's not just wood that he uses to work his magic. There are sculptures made from old motor parts and even a stove around the farm – permanent exhibits that exist beyond the ephemeral woodpile, which diminishes each year, as winter sets in. Some artists would be sad to see their hard work go up in flames, but not Gary. As the last logs from his *Starry Night* mosaic head to the wood burner he smiles. 'It was just another season, and just another woodpile.'

Gary uses wood from local tree species to create unique nature scenes each year.

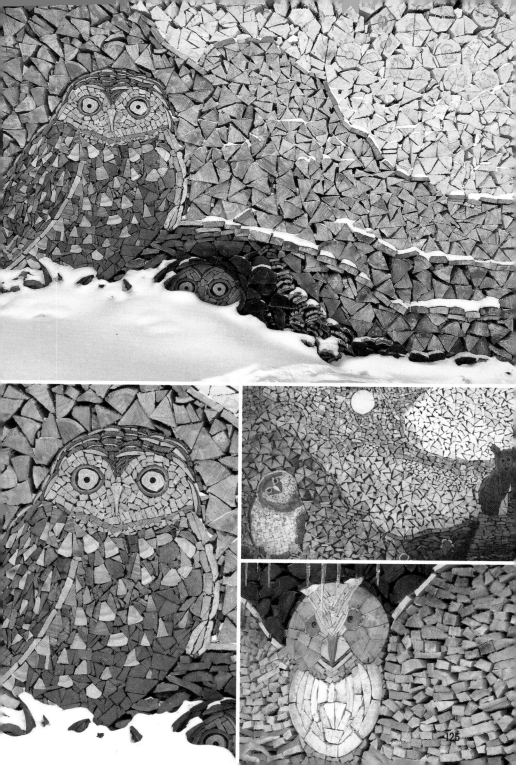

125

HOW TO

✗ TRAIN TO WIN ✗

Nobody climbs to the top of the lumberjack tree without shedding a little blood, a lot of sweat and even a few tears. But you can minimise the pain by making sure you train smart. Who better to put you through your paces than five-time British champion Elgan Pugh?

The UK's greatest axeman is living proof that to be the best at something, you don't need start doing it while you're in nappies. Unlike some of his contemporary athletes who inherited a lumber sports family legacy, the 38-year-old five-time winner of the British Stihl Timbersports Championships didn't swing an axe until he was 27, but he's been making up for lost time ever since.

'Growing up in Wales as a farmer's son, I used to love visiting the Royal Welsh Show every year with my parents,' recalls Elgan, speaking from his home in Bala, Wales, UK. 'I would watch the woodchopping displays for hours each year, but it wasn't until my late twenties that an axe demo team at another local show invited me to give it a go.'

As a trained carpenter and owner of a construction company, weighing in at a strong 90–95kg (198–209lb), Elgan was already in pretty good shape for lumber sports. After taking up the opportunity to join the Clwyd Axemen team for some training sessions, he soon discovered he also had the passion and talent he needed

to succeed. Just two months later, Elgan was back at 2009's Royal Welsh Show as a competitor, where he came second in the underhand chop event.

Entering his first national timbersports event in 2012, Elgan narrowly missed out on third place, which drove him to train harder. With no nationals in 2013, he focused on the 2014 competition, where he took silver. 'To come second so soon after I started competing was great, but I'd done a lot of preparation, so it wasn't really what I was after!' laughs Elgan. Upping his training game, he returned the following year to claim the championship title, which he has won every year the event has been held since.

'The thrill of competing is all I need to keep me motivated and working hard. During the off-season, I'll do more mountain biking, road cycling and weight training. In the months leading up to a competition, I'll spend hours practising each of the events,' says Elgan, who holds the British records for the stock saw, hot saw and Champion's Trophy competitions. 'I love having

A lumberjack competes in a woodchopping competition at an agricultural show in South Australia, 1917.

the opportunity to go up against some fantastic athletes. We're all competitive, but very supportive, too. It's a great sport to be part of.'

Staying at the top of the game takes commitment and discipline, and while it's competing that drives Elgan to train, setting fitness goals can help you to achieve your own personal bests, too. On the next page, Elgan shares some of his top training tips to get you in good shape, and remember: 'It's never too late to try something new, so go for it!'

WARM UP

'This is essential before you do any training. I'll go for a short jog, bike ride or do some skipping for five minutes to get my blood pumping. Then I'll do a variety of gentle arm swings and shoulder rolls to loosen up: 10–15 forwards, then the same in reverse.'

MUSCLE POWER

'I have a squat rack at home for weightlifting, and I do lots of dead lifts and squats – both great for building power. Try to include some squats and lunges in your workout to build up your leg muscles, adding a kettlebell or medicine ball for an extra challenge. Planks are great for working out your core, and side planks really strengthen your side muscles, which will help when you're chopping and sawing.'

BALL SLAM

'Start with the medicine ball on the floor. Squat down to pick it up and then quickly lift it up above your head, before slamming it down onto the ground in front of you, as hard as you can. Keep your back straight and your legs and elbows slightly bent.

You're aiming to improve your strength, stamina and speed, so repeat the movement as fast as possible. Start with a 5kg (11lb) ball and do around 10 repetitions, then slowly build up the ball weight and reps. I use a 6kg (13lb) ball and do around 50 slams each session. This means that when I come to lift a 3–3.5kg (7–8lb) axe in a competition, it feels a lot lighter.'

SHOULDER STRETCH

'This is an easy but effective exercise to really stretch out the muscles in your shoulders and arms. Use a weightlifting bar, or even a broom, and drape your arms over the pole, until you feel a good – but not painful – stretch. Slowly rotate the upper body from the hips as far as you can, then hold the position for 10 seconds. Now, slowly rotate back to the centre and then round to the other side, holding for another 10. This exercise isn't about speed or reps, but achieving a controlled, deep stretch.'

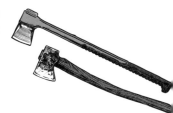

Before you start any new exercise routine, consult a medical professional. Increase weights and repetitions slowly, and always stop exercising and consult your doctor if you feel any pain.

KETTLE SWING

'Like the ball slam, this exercise will improve your chopping technique while giving you a full-body workout, but the movements are slower and more controlled. Start with the kettlebell on the ground in front of you and grip it in the way you would an axe, with your dominant hand at the top of the handle, and the other hand below it.

Next, swing the kettlebell up above your head, replicating the arc you'd make when swinging an axe, keeping your legs and elbows bent. Swing the bell back down to just between your legs, without letting it touch the ground, then take it straight back up again. I do between 50 to 100 repetitions and lift a 16kg (35lbs) kettlebell, but start with a weight you're comfortable with, and build up slowly.'

WIND DOWN

'Always leave some time to stretch properly after each training session, making sure you pay attention to your arm and leg muscles – you'll really appreciate this the next day.'

RECOVERY TIPS

'Eat a healthy diet, with lots of vitamins and minerals, to help keep you in tip-top shape. I also take a multivitamin and an omega-3 complex for joints to help keep them supple. Good hydration is key, so drink lots of water.'

TOP RIGHT: Elgan competes in the underhand chop competition at the 2018 Stihl Timbersports World Championship.
ABOVE: Elgan holds the British records in the stock saw, hot saw and Champions Trophy competitions.

SHANTY BOY SONGS

From melancholy Irish ballads to bawdy drinking ditties, lumberjacks loved to sing songs after a hard day's graft amid the pines. Fiddles at the ready ...

Drawing on work experiences, the dangers of the job, drinking and, of course, matters of the heart, lumberjack songs are as varied as those who wrote and sung them. European immigrants brought their music and tales to North America's logging camps, where lyrics were reworked to reflect the shanty boys' way of life. The lumberjacks also added bluegrass, Civil War songs and spirituals into the mix. Songs were sung in the evening beside the stove or campfire, as men sharpened axes, darned clothes, talked, told stories and played cards. Accompanied by instruments, including the fiddle, banjo, guitar, mouth organ and even a hand saw played with a bow, the songs travelled with the fellers as they moved camps evolving as they'd go.

Lumberjacks have continued to feature in music genres from country to rock and rap, inspiring Johnny Cash's '*Lumberjack*', Jackyl's '*The Lumberjack*' (which includes an actual chainsaw solo) and Serum featuring Inja's '*Lumberjackin*' – with Monty Python's '*The Lumberjack Song*' becoming a camp classic of a wholly irreverent kind.

In 2020, historic work songs made it into the mainstream, when #tiktokshanty went viral around the globe, thanks to the video-sharing platform, TikTok, with a 19th-century whaler's song, '*Wellerman*' – recorded by Scottish shanty-singing postman, Nathan Evans – topping the charts in early 2021. Think you could be the new #lumberjackshantysensation? Get TikTokking with these tunes.

ABOVE: The Beneway Beneway Camp Orchestra poses for a group photo in Montmorency County, Michigan, US, 1900.

ONCE MORE A-LUMBERING GO

Traditional lumbertale 'Once More a-Lumbering Go' was first featured in John S Springer's 1851 book *Forest Life and Forest Trees*, under the title 'The Logger's Boast'.

Recordings include a version by lumberjack Carl Lathrop recorded by Alan Lomaxe in 1938, another by 'The Adirondack Minstrel' Lawrence Older from the 1960s and a recent take by Minnesotan singer and musician Brian Miller.

Come all you sons of freedom and listen
  to my theme
Come all you roving lumberjacks that run
  the Saginaw stream
We'll cross the Tittabawassee where the
  mighty waters flow
And we'll roam the wild woods over and
  once more a-lumbering go

[Chorus]
And once more a-lumbering go
And we'll range the wild woods over
And once more a-lumbering go

When the white frost hits the valley,
  and the snow conceals the woods
The lumberjack has enough to do to find
  his family food
No time he has for pleasure or to hunt
  the buck and doe
He will roam the wild woods over and
  once more a-lumbering go

[Repeat chorus]

With our crosscut saws and axes we will
  make the woods resound
And many a tall and stately tree will
  come crashing to the ground

With cant hooks on our shoulders to our
  boot tops deep in snow
We will roam the wild woods over and
  once more a-lumbering go

[Repeat chorus]

You may talk about your farms,
  your houses and fine places
But pity not the shanty boys while
  dashing on their sleigh
For around the good campfire at night
  we'll sing while wild winds blow
And we'll roam the wild woods over and
  once more a-lumbering go

[Repeat chorus]

Then when navigation opens and the
  water runs so free
We'll drive our logs to Saginaw once
  more our girls to see
They will all be there to welcome us and
  our hearts in rapture flow
We will stay with them through summer
  the once more a-lumbering go

[Repeat chorus]

When our youthful days are ended and
  our stories are growing old
We'll take to us each man a wife and
  settle on the farm
We'll have enough to eat and drink,
  contented we will go
We will tell our wives of our hard times
  and no more a-lumbering go

And no more a-lumbering go
We will tell our wives of our hard times
And no more a-lumbering go

LUMBERJACK'S ALPHABET

The 'Lumberjack's Alphabet' was a favourite song in the camps, with each logger putting their own unique spin on the shanty. 'P for Peerless' refers to the brand of chewing tobacco that was popular with the men.

A is for axe which we swing to and fro
B is for boys that handle them so
C is for cant hooks, the logs we make spin
D is for danger that we're always in

[Chorus]
And so merry, so merry, so merry are we
We are the boys when we're out on a spree
Sing 'hi-derry col-derry, hi-derry-dum'
Give the lumberjacks whisky and nothing goes wrong!

E is for echo which through the
   woods rang
F is for foreman that pushes our gang
G is for grinding stone, the axes we ground
H is for handle that turns them around

[Repeat chorus]

I is for ink which our letters we've wrote
J is for jacket we wore for a coat
K is for kindling, the fires we'd light
L is for lice that bothers by night

[Repeat chorus]

M is for money, which everyone owes
N is for needle that patches our clothes
O is for oxen the road we swung through
P is for Peerless, which everyone chews

[Repeat chorus]

Q is for quiet, when we are asleep
R is for rabbits which everyone eats
S is for sleigh, so stout and strong
T is for teams that tote them along

[Repeat chorus]

U is for use which we put ourselves to
V is for valley, we tramp it right through
W is the woods we leave in the spring
And now I have sung all I'm going to sing

BAND ON THE BALL

Formed in 1921, the Lumberjack Band was a marching band that played at the games of the Green Bay Packers, the NFL team from Wisconsin. They earned their name from rocking the lumberjack style in plaid mackinaw jackets, heavy boots and hunting caps.

A man wanders amidst the felled trees of the forests of Cowlitz County, Washington, US, 1941.

'He's a Lumberjack and he's OK!' Members of Monty Python, and actor Tom Hanks, perform at The Concert For George at the Royal Albert Hall, London, UK, 2002.

THE LUMBERJACK SONG

Perhaps the world's most famous wood-felling anthem, 'The Lumberjack Song' first appeared in a 1969 episode of *Monty Python's Flying Circus*, featuring the iconic clip of cross-dressing logger Michael Palin, an increasingly concerned chorus of Canadian Mounties and girlfriend Connie Booth, who bemoans: 'Oh, Bevis! And I thought you were so butch!'

I'm a lumberjack and I'm OK
I sleep all night and I work all day
I cut down trees
I eat my lunch
I go to the lavatory

On Wednesdays I go shopping and have
  buttered scones for tea

I'm a lumberjack and I'm OK
I sleep all night and I work all day
I cut down trees
I skip and jump
I like to press wild flowers
I put on women's clothing and hang
  around in bars

I'm a lumberjack and I'm OK
I sleep all night and I work all day
I cut down trees
I wear high heels, suspenders and a bra
I wish I'd been a girlie just like my
  dear Papa!

LUMBERJACK LINGO

If you want to live the life of a lumberjack, you'll need to know your pike pole from your peavey. Use these words and phrases to help you up your logging game. Yo-ho!

ALL HANDS AND THE COOK
Similar to the nautical 'all hands on deck'. Used to summon help for an emergency, such as a major log jam

AMEN CORNER
A place in the bunkhouse for storytelling

ANTIFREEZE
Any alcoholic drink

AXLE GREASE OR SKID GREASE
Butter

BAIT CAN OR BEAN CAN
A lunch bucket

BARKED
Someone who's lost their hair

BAR TOAD OR BAR FLY
Someone who spends lots of time in saloons

BEAN BURNER, BELLY-ROBBER OR BOILER
A bad cook

BEAR STORY
A tall story

BEAR WALLOW
A dirty or untidy bunk

BEAVER
A clumsy axeman, or a rough and uneven cut of wood

BETWEEN THE ROCK AND THE RIVER
Caught in a difficult situation with no chance of escape

BIRLING
Log rolling

BLACKJACK OR MUD
Coffee

BLANKET FEVER
An affliction suffered by lazy lumberjacks

BOILING-UP SHACK
A place to bathe or do laundry

BOOM
Logs chained or tied together end-to-end, used to catch and corral logs on the river

BOX UP THE DOUGH
To cook

BUCKER
Someone who saws trees into logs

BULL COOK
A boy who does chores around the camp, including feeding livestock and sweeping the bunkhouse

CALKS OR CORKS
Short, sharp spikes set in the soles and heels of shoes, used for better footing on logs during the river drive

CANT HOOK
A long pole with a thimble and a large, levered hook at the end, used to turn and roll logs

CHOKER SETTER
A logger who attaches cables to felled logs before they're hauled

COOKEE
A cook's helper

COUGAR DEN
A bunkhouse

DAYLIGHT IN THE SWAMP!
A saying used to wake up sleeping loggers

DEVIL'S CUP
A tin cup without a handle that becomes hot when filled with tea or coffee

DONKEY ENGINE OR STEAM DONKEY
A steam-powered winch used for hauling logs, operated by an engineer known as a 'donkeyman' or 'donkey puncher'

EPSOM SALTS OR IODINE
The logging camp doctor

FALLER
A lumberjack who cuts down trees

FLUNKEY
Someone who serves meals in the logging camp

FLY BREAD
Raisin bread

OPPOSITE: A logging crew sits on a giant sequoia in Humboldt County, California, US, 1905. **ABOVE:** A choker attaches a choker loop to a log before a donkey engine winches it from the woods to the landing area in Cowlitz County, Washington, US, 1941.

This load of logs was the largest ever hauled on sleds by horses, Pine Island, Minnesota, US, 1909.

PIKE POLE
A long wooden pole with a straight metal spike and hook at the end, used to control logs on the river and construct log rafts

ROAD MONKEYS
Crews that maintain logging routes and shovel the horse manure

SAWYERS
A pair of loggers who fell trees together

SHANTY BOY
A logger

SHANTY QUEEN
A logger's wife who lives in a rustic shack

SHAPE UP OR SHIP OUT
What the boss says to lazy loggers

SHOEPACK PIE
A pie made from vinegar, cornflour, sugar and lemon or vanilla

SKIDDER
A heavy vehicle, used to transport felled trees from the logging site

SKOOKUM
A strong or brave man

SKUNK BIT
Stinking drunk

GABRIEL HORN
A tin horn used to announce meals were ready

GROUNDHOG
Someone who guides logs onto sleds

HASHHOUSE
The cookhouse

LOGGING BERRIES
Stewed prunes

LOG SCALER
The person who records the quantity and quality of felled logs before they're taken to the sawmill

MACARONI
Sawdust

MISERY WHIP
A crosscut saw, used by two lumberjacks for cutting trees

MONKEY BLANKETS, STOVE LIDS OR SWEAT PADS
Pancakes

NOSE BAG
Cold lunch eaten in the woods

PASS THE 44S
Pass the beans

PEAVEY
A long wooden pole with a metal spike and pivoting hooked arm at the end, used to lift and turn logs on a river drive

SNAKE ROOM
A room in a bar where drunken lumberjacks go to sleep off a hangover

SOUNDS LIKE A BUZZSAW IN A NUT
A heavy snorer

SWAMPWATER
Tea

SWEDISH FIDDLE
A crosscut saw

SWINGDINGLE
A sleigh for hauling food to loggers in the woods

TAR
Bad coffee

TEAMSTER
Someone who looks after and drives the oxen or horses used to pull logs

TIMBER
The warning cry of the faller, just before a tree goes down

TIMBER BEAST
Anyone who works in the woods

TIN PANTS
Heavy waterproof trousers worn by loggers

TOP LOADERS
The highly paid and skilled men in charge of loading and hauling sleds

WHISTLE PUNK
The person who passes signals from the choker setter to the donkey engineer when logs are ready to be winched

WIDOW MAKER
A dead limb on a tree overhead

YO-HO!
Used to cheer on other lumberjacks at work or in competitions

---

WORD UP
American lumberjack, historian and writer Stewart Holbrook wrote a handy Logger's Dictionary, published in his book *Holy Old Mackinaw: A Natural History of the American Lumberjack* in 1938.

Buckers use a crosscut saw on a felled tree in Malheur National Forest, Grant County, Oregon, US, 1942.

BIBLIOGRAPHY

App, Jerry. *When the White Pine Was King: A History of Lumberjacks, Loggers, Log Drives, and Sawdust Cities in Wisconsin.* Madison, WI: Wisconsin Historical Society, 2020.

Atlantic Canada Tourism Partnership. Accessed March 30, 2021. atlanticcanadaholiday.co.uk.

Australian Axeman's Hall of Fame and Timberworks. Accessed March 30, 2021. thaiimperiallatrobe.com.au.

Beard, G. M. 'Remarks Upon Jumpers or Jumping Frenchmen'. *Journal of Nervous and Mental Disease* 5 (1878): 623–640. 'Experiments with the Jumpers of Maine'. *Popular Science Monthly* 18 (1880): 170–178.

Beck, E. C., ed. *Songs of the Michigan Lumberjacks: From the Archive of Folk Song.* Recorded by Alan Lomax and Harry B. Welliver. Washington, DC: Library of Congress, 1960.

Burg, Rob. *A Taste of the North Country.* Last accessed March 30, 2021. atasteofthenorthcountry. wordpress.com.

Center for Sustainable Economy. Accessed March 30, 2021. sustainable-economy.org.

Conlin, Joseph R. 'A Social History of Food in Logging Camps'. *Journal of Forest History* 23, no. 4 (October 1974): 164–185.

Cox, William T. Illustrated by Du Bois, Coert. *Fearsome Creatures of the Lumberwoods: With a Few Desert and Mountain Beasts.* Washington, DC: Press of Judd & Detweiler, Inc., 1910.

Curry, Kevin. Fit Men Cook. Accessed March 30, 2021. fitmencook.com.

Destination Canada. Accessed March 30, 2021. destinationcanada.com.

Discover New England. Accessed March 30, 2021. discovernewengland.org.

Early Logging on the Menominee Indian Reservation: Life and Lore of the Menominee Lumberjacks Menominee Indian Tribe of Wisconsin Historic Preservation Department, 2012.

Edmonds, Michael. *Out of the Northwoods: The Many Lives of Paul Bunyan.* Madison, WI: Historical Society Press, 2009.

Ellis, Charles. 'Among the Michigan Pines'. *The Chicago Current,* Vol. III, 1885.

Fitzmaurice, John W. *The Shanty Boy or Life in a Lumber Camp.* Cheboygan, MI: Steam Democrat Press, 1889.

Foat, Joanna. *Lumberjills: Britain's Forgotten Army.* Cheltenham, UK: The History Press, 2019.

Forest History Society. Accessed March 30, 2021. foresthistory.org.

Forest Stewardship Council (FSC). Accessed March 30, 2021. fsc.org/en.

Forestry and Land Scotland. Accessed March 30, 2021. forestryandland.gov.scot.

Fryeburg Fair. Accessed March 30, 2021. fryeburgfair.org.

Great Lakes USA. Accessed March 30, 2021. greatlakesusa.co.uk.

Holbrook, Stewart H. *Holy Old Mackinaw: A Natural History of the American Lumberjack*. New York: Macmillian Company, 1938.

Johnny Appleseed Festival. Accessed March 30, 2021. johnnyappleseedfest.net.

Kearney, Lakeshore. *The Hodag and Other Tales of the Logging Camps*. Madison, WI: Democrat Printing Company, 1928.

La French Sarah. Accessed March 30, 2021. lafrenchsarah.com.

La Drave. Directed by Raymond Garceau. Montreal: National Film Board of Canada, 1957.

Laurel Fork Sapsuckers Sugar Camp. Accessed March 30, 2021. laurelforksapsuckers.com.

Lumberjack Beard Company. Accessed March 30, 2021. lumberjackbeardcompany.com

Lumberjack World Championships. Accessed March 30, 2021. lumberjackworldchampionships.com.

Maine Office of Tourism. Accessed March 30, 2021. visitmaine.com.

Melvin, J. I. "Foresters." *Meet the Members: A Record of the Timber Corps of the Women's Land Army*. Bristol, UK: Bennett Brothers, 1945.

Menominee Historic Preservation Department, Wisconsin menominee-nsn.gov Imperial War Museum Dept of Printed Books.

Minnesota Tourism. Accessed March 30, 2021. exploreminnesota.com.

BIBLIOGRAPHY

Muir, John. 'God's First Temples: How Shall We Preserve Our Forests?' *Sacramento Record Union*, 1876.

National Film Board of Canada. Accessed March 30, 2021. nfb.ca/film/log_drivers_waltz. nfb.ca/film/log_drive.

New York State Woodsmen's Field Days. Accessed March 30, 2021. woodsmensfielddays.com.

Nova Scotia Tourism. Accessed March 30, 2021. novascotia.com.

NYCitySlab. Accessed March 30, 2021. nycityslab.com.

Pike, Robert E. *Tall Trees, Tough Men: A Vivid, Anecdotal History of Logging and Log-Driving in New England*. New York: W. W. Norton, 1967.

Simmons, Amelia. *American Cookery*. Hartford, Connecticut: Hudson & Goodwin, 1796.

Springer, John S. 'Once More a-Lumbering Go / The Logger's Boast'. *Forest Life and Forest Trees*. New York: Harper & Brothers, 1851.

Squamish Days Loggers Sports Festival. Accessed March 30, 2021. squamishdays.ca.

Stewart, K. Bernice, and Homer A. Watt. *Legends of Paul Bunyan, Lumberjack*. Vol. XVII of *Transactions of the Wisconsin Academy of Sciences*. Madison, WI: The Wisconsin Academy of Sciences, Arts, and Letters, 1916.

STIHL TIMBERSPORTS®. Accessed March 30, 2021. stihl-timbersports.com.

Sustainable Forestry Initiative (SFI). Accessed March 30, 2021. forests.org.

Sydney Royal Easter Show. Accessed March 30, 2021. eastershow.com.au.

The Lumberjack Song written & composed by Michael Palin, Terry Jones & Fred Tomlinson, issued under license from Universal Music Publishing Ltd. on behalf of Python Monty Pictures Ltd.

Timber Lounge. Accessed March 30, 2021. timberlounge.ca.

Tourism New Brunswick. Accessed March 30, 2021. tourismnewbrunswick.ca.

Travel Yukon. Accessed March 30, 2021. travelyukon.com.

Tryon, Henry H. *Fearsome Critters*. Cornwall, NY: Idlewild Press, 1939.

US Bureau of Labor Statistics. Accessed March 30, 2021. https://www.bls.gov/news.release/pdf/cfoi.pdf - page 3 chart.

Wild Axe Productions. Accessed March 30, 2021. wildaxe.com.

Wisconsin Tourism. Accessed March 30, 2021. travelwisconsin.com.

PICTURE CREDITS

PICTURE CREDITS

ABOUT THE AUTHOR

Lauren Jarvis is an editor, writer and photographer specialising in adventure, wildlife and conservation. She has travelled extensively around North America and the world, enjoying such challenges as tracking grizzlies in British Columbia and trekking to Everest Base Camp. A regular contributor to *National Geographic*, Lauren is passionate about the planet's wild places and animals and loves spending time in the woods. Follow her on Instagram @laurenjarvistravels.

THE AUTHOR WOULD LIKE TO THANK

Darren Hudson at Wild Axe Productions, Nova Scotia; Stanley Scott, Nova Scotia; Hayward Meisner, Ironworks, Nova Scotia; Jethro Wood, Cloak & Dagger Tattoo Parlour, London; The Stihl Timbersports Press Team; Eben Lehmen, Director of Library & Archives; Finn Partners / The Brighter Group; Click Travel Marketing and PR; Travel and Tourism Marketing (TTM); US Forest Service; US National Park Service; Visit USA; Virginia Tourism; Travel Wisconsin; Walking Art Tattoos; Webster County; Woolrich. And her family. . . for helping her to see the forest for the trees.

'And into the forest I go, to lose my mind and find my soul'

JOHN MUIR

First published 2021 by Ammonite Press
an imprint of Guild of Master Craftsman
Publications Ltd, Castle Place,
166 High Street, Lewes, East Sussex,
BN7 1XU, United Kingdom

ISBN 978-1-78145-445-9

A catalogue record for this book is available
from the British Library

Publisher Jonathan Grogan
Copy Editors Susie Duff, Jane Roe
Production Manager Jim Bulley
Designer Claire Stevens

Colour origination by GMC Reprographics
Printed and bound in China

AMMONITE
PRESS

ammonitepress.com

FSC
www.fsc.org
MIX
Paper from
responsible sources
FSC® C144853